CHOICES

CHOICES

Taking Control of Your Life and Making It Matter

MELODY BEATTIE

HarperOne
An Imprint of HarperCollinsPublishers

HarperOne

HarperCollins books may be purchased for educational, business, or sales promotional use. For information please write: Special Markets Department, HarperCollins Publishers, 10 East 53rd Street, New York, NY 10022.

HarperCollins Web site: http://www.harpercollins.com
HarperCollins®, 📖®, and HarperOne™ are trademarks of HarperCollins Publishers.

FIRST HARPERCOLLINS PAPERBACK EDITION PUBLISHED IN 2003

Library of Congress Cataloging-in-Publication Data
Beattie, Melody.
Choices : taking control of your life and making it matter /
Melody Beattie.
p. cm.
Includes index.
ISBN 978-0-06-050722-0
1. Spiritual life. 2. Success. I. Title.
BL624.B43   2002
170'.44—dc21   200202380

10 11 12 13 RRD(H) 16 15 14

For us.

Contents

—————

Open Your Present

"When you figure out the secret to absolute control in every situation while maintaining mental wholeness, I would love to know," a woman said to me one day. That's what this book is about: how to take control of our lives without going subtly or profoundly insane.

"My friend is twenty-four; engaged to be married. Her boyfriend went skiing this weekend and was killed. Why did he have to die? Why does she have to go through this?"

"I dated a man for three months. Fell in love for the first time in years. Then he dumped me. It was the first time I'd opened my heart since my divorce. Why did that happen to me?"

Why did my husband cheat on me and ruin our marriage? Why is my new car a lemon? Why did such a saintly woman have to spend the last seven years of her life paralyzed and confined to bed? Why has my child turned on me? Why won't my last boyfriend let go of me? Why can't I let go—really let go—of him? Why are my parents insane?

It's easy to suggest *Get a grip, Don't be a victim, There's a reason things happen* when the problem happens to someone else. Harder when we're the one feeling afraid, guilty, angry, hurt, bewildered, staring our loss and emotions in the face.

What are the situations that cause us to feel like we're out of control? When we try to do something we can't. When things don't go as we hoped or planned.

Whenever we can't see the game of cause and effect at play we feel confused, frustrated, and vulnerable to forces we don't comprehend. *Is it random chaos?* we wonder. *Or is there really some sort of Plan?* Or, like C. S. Lewis in *A Grief Observed,* we may believe clearly in God and the Plan. "The conclusion I dread is not 'So there's no God after all,'" Lewis wrote, "but 'So this is what God's really like.'"

Is everything predetermined, or do we actually have free will? Both ideas are true. We can't choose what's on television, but we can choose what channel to watch or whether to watch television at all. This process of discerning what we can choose—what we do have control over—and what we can't is the heart of mental health and the heart of the spiritual path.

A lot of things will happen to us over which we have no control. That includes other people, their use of free will (or not), and acts of God and life. We do have control over something, and that is our own behavior and our power of choice. We can't control what happens to us, but yes, we can choose.

Do our choices really matter? Do we really have any, other than what we're going to eat for breakfast and lunch? What about when things happen that we can't control? The person we love most goes away—either he or she dies, leaves, or we break up with him or her to save our own lives. Our best friend lies to us, betrays us. Or a parent or best friend gets sick.

What choices do we have now?

Or we find ourselves alone, raising two young children with no child support and a low-paying job. Or we're forty-eight years old and still living alone without a shred of hope left about meeting Mr. or Ms. Right. Maybe our business goes broke and our hopes crumble. Or that project we've put our whole life into just won't materialize. We try and try but can't get our dream off the ground.

We might have choices, but we can't see what they are.

A friend of my daughter's sat in my kitchen with me one day about three months after my son, Shane, died. I was trying to keep moving. It was tough. My daily goal was just to get out of bed. She touched my shoulder, looked into my eyes.

"We had to write an essay about courage in English class today," she said. "So I wrote about you."

Her words touched my heart; they also frustrated me.

I wasn't brave. Life hadn't given me a choice.

Or maybe I just didn't like the options I had: *keep going or quit.*

Sometimes we feel that we don't have any choice—at least none that we can see yet. Or we think we have to act the way we feel. Sometimes our only options are choices we don't like—neither one is preferred, but one is unacceptable—a situation known as a *hard call*. Other times we see so many options indecision paralyzes our mind.

We don't choose—which is making a choice.

Or we'd rather have someone else choose for us; then we don't have to take responsibility for the results. Well, we do—we have to take responsibility for the choices we've allowed someone to make on our behalf.

Not all choices are black and white. Some are gray. Emotions and extenuating circumstances may be involved. And our challenges— the ones requiring hard or tough calls—usually happen at the place we would least prefer that they occurred. Our weakest link. Some of the choices we label mistakes turn out to be the best things we could have done. Other times our noblest gestures backfire, hurting others and racking up more consequences for them and us.

Gaining control of our lives takes awareness and focused intention, like climbing a flight of steep steps. How much power do we have? Less than many of us hoped for, but more than we think. By using our free will, we can take part in shaping our lives no matter what life throws our way.

Consciously or not, we've been doing it all along.

It's not what recovering alcoholics call an *easier softer road* or *self-will run riot,* this business of focusing our will and climbing up steep steps. Using our free will to make enlightened choices often means making the truly hard calls such as letting go of cherished ideas, trusting God, and having faith even when doing so hurts and flies in the face of what we can see with our eyes. Other times it means doing some work ourselves. Usually it's a combination of both.

The great irony of control is this: usually when we're out of control, we don't see it. We just see that others are spinning around. In an odd way, when we're in control of ourselves, even the bizarre seems to be part of a plan.

Most of us have had moments when everything falls into place. We've been willing to let go, trust, surrender—even though we don't know what the outcome will be. Then something magical and wonderful happens, confirming our faith. We feel like we've discovered fire, and like we've discovered it for the first time.

Gee, I really can trust God, we think. And we think that not because we get what we want, because as most of us know that can be an illusion. We think that because for that moment we feel the order, the aliveness, the connectedness. The Reason behind things happening shows its face.

If you want more of those moments, this book is for you. This book is for ordinary people age 13 to 103 who want intimate relationships with themselves, other people, and the world.

We'll look at some simple secrets about how this world works, and how to apply those ideas to the choices we make each day.

We'll draw from the well of religions, some of the great minds, and stories from real people's lives. Some of these stories for various reasons will be fictionalized or portrayed anonymously; others will be told almost exactly as they occurred. I'll weave snippets into this from the three months I spent in China and Tibet.

Usually when I write a book there is one core experience at the heart of it. Many people's experiences will be in here. And the experiences aren't always one dramatic incident in time; many stories depict the gritty choices people make each day that affect the course of their lives. These stories tell a larger story about living life consciously aware that we are guided by God.

This is a handbook for reminding us we have choices and the ability to choose—even when it feels like we don't—and exploring what some of these choices are. In reality many more choices are available than the ones presented here. By reading the stories, you'll be able to translate that to the situations in your life and grow in consciousness about the choices you face and make each day.

You can read the stories according to what you need at a particular time. Or you can read them from front to back like a regular book. The important idea is to translate the concept of choosing into the everyday details of *your* life.

It can be easy to see choices available to other people. But sometimes it's more difficult to see and act on the choices presented to each one of us, each day.

Sometimes life feels like a mushy swamp of horrific incidents that we're wandering through wearing concrete boots. Some of us have learned coping devices along the way. We make choices that keep us numb, help us deal with extraordinarily painful situations, create a lot of drama—but don't really get us what we want and where we want to go in our lives.

Sometimes we get confused. Our emotions block our ability to clearly think things through. Just a small wake-up call is all that's often needed to remind us how powerful our choices are and what a difference the small choices we make each day can make in the course and the quality of our lives.

Wake up. The alarm clock just went off. Whether we use it or not, we've been given a gift. We can duck it and dodge it, blame our behaviors on our parents or on God's will. But it sets us apart from angels, this ability we've been given to choose.

It's like having a wonderful birthday present wrapped, sitting in the corner of the room, then forgetting it's there. Go ahead. Unwrap it. Take it out and use it.

The gift of free will is for you.

Section I

———

THE GREAT LAW

We're at the beach. Splashes of lavender and pink begin to color the sky. Then that big orange ball drops out of sight. It looks like it's dropped into the sea.

Oh, the sun is setting, we say. But the sun isn't setting. It's standing still. We're spinning away from it at a thousand miles an hour.

There's more to life than what we think, more than we can see with our eyes. Some things are true whether we see and believe them or not. Things aren't always as they appear.

There's an old story circulating in writers' circles. It's about a writer who lived in the outer regions of Alaska a long time ago. One day he decided to take a journey to a place called *New York*. He made the trip, then came back to his people. He wanted to tell them everything he had seen: "They have skyscrapers. Airplanes. Vehicles that go very fast and don't need dogs to pull them. Things that you can't imagine or comprehend I have seen."

The people in his hometown pooh-poohed him. They couldn't imagine it, so they thought he was lying, making it all up. The writer took another trip to New York. When he came back this time, he used a different approach.

"It's okay there," he said. "They have a couple roads and it's a little warmer. No big deal."

Well, when he said this all the people oohed and aahed. He had told them something they could comprehend, something their minds could take in, something that was palatable and digestible enough for them to believe.

If someone told us we could have the life of our dreams by harnessing our gift of free will, we'd laugh them off. At least, I know I would. It would be more than I could believe.

If someone came along and told us we could make our lives a little bit better by thinking about the choices we made each day and then using our gift of free will to steer a slightly different course, we'd probably agree.

So, by understanding the law of cause and effect and the power you have to choose, you can improve your life a little bit.

But the truth is, you can change things a lot.

"Meldid, come with me," my Tibetan guide, Lami, said toward the end of my trip to Tibet. (He couldn't say *Melody*, so he called me *Meldid* instead.)

He dragged me through dug-up city streets into a monastery in Lhasa. Three monks were sitting on cushions in the corner. Another monk was helping a woman, probably in her thirties, shake a container of sticks until some of the sticks wiggled out and fell onto the floor.

The container of sticks reminded me of a large version of Pick Up Sticks, a children's game I used to play.

"What's she doing?" I asked Lami.

"Shhh. Watch carefully," he said. "She's having her fortune told."

The monk looked solemnly at the way the sticks had fallen, then led the woman to the corner, to the cluster of fortune-telling monks.

"Tibetan scriptures contain both knowledge and wisdom," Lami said. "They hold all information for everything in our world—past, future, and present—from how to build an airplane to what to do about a problem with a child.

"From the way her sticks fell, the monks will pick a scripture. That verse will answer her question."

I can only guess what question the woman asked the monks. She looked weighted down, concerned, sad. Was her relationship going to work? Were her finances going to improve? Was her child going to be okay? Was someone she trusted betraying her now or would he or she do it again? Was an ill family member or friend going to recover or die? Was her own health going to improve? Was life going to bring her more of what she wanted and less of what she didn't, or would it be the other way around?

Whatever the monks told her about her fate didn't make her feel better. They consoled her, but she looked sadder and more distraught when she left.

Now it was my turn to see what the scriptures had to say.

I shook the container of sticks. Then the monks talked to Lami, chattering in a language I didn't understand. Lami turned to me.

"The scriptures say it is very important that you do only what you choose."

I rolled the words around in my head several times. Did the monks mean I had carte blanche, an open ticket to life? Did they mean I shouldn't surrender my free will to anyone but God? *Oh, I get it,* I thought later, still mulling over those words. *I can do whatever I want. Anyone can.* But that wasn't what they meant.

The monks were saying, "Honor the gift of free will, and be aware of the Great Law of Cause and Effect."

For every action force there is a corresponding reaction force which is equal in magnitude and opposite in direction. Sir Isaac Newton identified the law, but it doesn't apply just to the world of science. It applies to our behaviors and choices and the spiritual realm, too.

We don't just get our choice; we get the consequence that choice creates.

Sometimes the choices we make are inconsequential. They create no significant results one way or the other. We go to bed at nine o'clock or ten. No big deal. But most of the choices we make don't affect just us; they create consequences that affect other people too.

There's a ripple effect, like dropping a pebble into a pond.

In the 1960s a mathematician and meteorologist, Edward Lorenz, made a discovery that wasn't new: no matter how hard they tried, the best meteorologists couldn't accurately predict the weather. This wasn't because there was unexplained chaos taking place in the atmosphere and the world. The unpredictable nature of things was due to forces that either couldn't be seen or that people had overlooked. These small causes could stop a storm that was brewing or create one that wasn't foreseen.

At first Lorenz thought it took a seagull flapping its wings to create a ripple in the weather pond. Then he changed his theory to what is now popularly known as the *Butterfly Effect.*

If enough butterflies in China flapped their wings, that flapping could eventually create turbulence that would cause a storm in the United States. There was order in the world. But we couldn't always see that order because there were more causes and effects taking place than we could see with our eyes and understand with our minds.

Given enough time to garner force, the smallest causes could evolve and create a big effect—interfering with or changing what was observable and what we predicted was going to occur.

Sometimes it's easy to see what causes what. Other times we look around, scratch our heads, and say, "What caused that?"

The answer may not be in plain view, but it's simple. *Whether we see it or not, a force occurred that created it. Somewhere way far away a butterfly flapped its wings.*

Small decisions—sometimes with predictable consequences and sometimes seemingly inconsequential—can alter our fate and the destiny of the world. One choice with enough butterflies flapping their wings thrown in can be the gateway to heaven or hell.

With so much riding on our choices, why doesn't someone just tell us the right thing to do and which choices to make? Why doesn't someone just hit us over the head with a stick when we do something wrong and drop a cookie in our laps when we do right? Why can't we immediately foresee the result of each decision we make?

"If we lived in a world where the effects of negative action were immediately manifested as pain and suffering, the element of choice would disappear from our lives," wrote Michael Berg in *The Way.*

We'd be like trained monkeys trying to get the cookie or avoid the stick.

Cause and effect—and the illusion of space in between—safeguards our gift of free will.

This section contains stories that illustrate how the Great Law of Cause and Effect works. As you read the stories about choices people have made, don't just feel how it feels to be them. We may say we're connected to everything and everyone in this world, but we can't connect to the world around us unless we first connect to ourselves.

Remember, there's more to life than what we think.

Feel how it feels to be you.

She Wanted a Baby

"C'mon honey. Hurry up," he said, starting the car.

Sherry climbed in, and laid her head back on the seat. She was tired—and big. Six months pregnant and painting homes wasn't easy. But she was happier than she'd been for a long time.

Sherry was young—only sixteen. Probably too young to be pregnant and starting a family. But it was all she wanted. She had met him in a drug ward. She had gone AWOL; he had stayed to complete treatment. One foster home after another had left her with only one dream—to have a family of her own, some people in her life that would stay, that she could love.

They had lived with his family for a while. Now they had a little hole-in-the-wall apartment. But it was theirs. They worked together during the day—painting and cleaning apartments, making enough money for food and bills.

She dozed off.

When she woke up, she was in an ambulance. He had hit a series of parked cars when he exited the off-ramp.

"Years later, I would realize that he didn't get sober. That I had gotten into a car with someone who was high. I didn't know it then," Sherry said. "At least not consciously."

The doctors at the hospital checked her, said she and the baby were fine, then released her. Two months later, her baby was born—a month early.

"At first the doctors just thought my daughter was slow. And had seizures," Sherry said. "That's what I told the social worker who came around when Candy was five. She's just a little slow, I said."

"The truth was, she couldn't feed herself. Sit up. Crawl. Say mama. She couldn't then, and she would never be able to. The only thing she's ever learned to do is hold up her head," Sherry said.

"The accident separated her from the placenta, causing seizures—and retardation. They said she wouldn't live very long. She's twenty-seven years old and has lived in an institution since she was five.

"Getting into that car—and what that did to my daughter and me—is something I've had to live with every day of my life."

I was standing in my daughter's kitchen, cutting tomatoes for a salad. I was watching her try to teach her son Julian that the stove was hot, and not to touch it. I watched her devoting her life to protecting her child.

"What are you thinking about, Mom?" she asked.

"I'm just standing here feeling guilty because I didn't protect my son enough. I feel responsible for letting him go skiing. That decision ended his life."

My answer surprised me, because it was like quiet background music playing constantly in my mind. I wasn't consciously aware it was there until I opened my mouth.

"Don't be silly. It was an accident," she said.

"Yeah, I know," I said. "But that doesn't change how I feel."

Many of us have made decisions we regret. That one decision alters the course of our lives. We don't get to go back; our challenge is living with life as it has evolved.

Sometimes these decisions are part of a larger problem, like alcoholism.

Other times, it's the hand of fate. Somebody else or a circumstance chose how it was going to be for another person—or for us.

Maybe we should teach our children more than "Don't touch that stove, it's hot." Maybe we should add, "Karma, baby. Remember the Great Law of Cause and Effect."

———

The easy part is getting forgiveness from God.
All we have to do is sincerely ask.
The hard part is forgiving others and
forgiving ourselves.

A Sad Week in Coventry

———

It was a solemn week in Coventry, England, in 1969.

Two local boys—Billy and Kenneth—died three days apart. Rev. Simon Stephens was young, only twenty-three. He was assistant to the chaplain at the hospital where the boys had died. While talking to Billy's parents, Father Stephens mentioned that another boy, Kenneth, had recently died. He mentioned Billy's death to Kenneth's parents, too.

It was a small gesture, a small choice.

The Lawleys, Kenneth's parents, sent flowers to Billy's funeral. Then Billy's folks and Kenneth's folks decided to get together to have tea and share memories about their sons.

It pleased Father Stephens that the parents were meeting. They were able to help each other, and in the process help themselves as well.

The parents continued to get together for informal talks and tea. Grieving a child can take a long time. As time passed, Father Stephens suggested that they open their little get-togethers to other people. Billy's folks and Kenneth's folks agreed.

It wasn't long before another couple joined their meetings.

By the year 2001, six hundred meetings were going on in the United States to help parents of the 225,000 children and young adults who die in this country each year. Hundreds more were taking place in twelve countries around the world. They were nondenominational and free. The Society of Compassionate Friends had officially begun.

Sometimes what helps the most is talking to people going through the same thing.

A series of small choices three people made one week in Coventry, England, changed the world.

We try so hard for that big brass ring—that peak moment of success, that great impact on the world. And when we try to make it happen, we usually get frustrated because we can't.

Most of the things we do that rock the world in a positive way start out with quiet choices that we have a good feeling about—sending that card, making that phone call—the small, pure things we do from our hearts, the things we do from love.

One of the best feelings in the world is feeling like our efforts are guided and blessed by God—when we make a choice that works. That usually doesn't happen when we're reaching for the brass ring. It happens when we're holding our hand out to help somebody else.

"When seasoned grievers reach out to the newly bereaved, energy that has been directed inward begins to flow outward and both are helped to heal," reports The Compassionate Friends.

This principle doesn't apply just to people going through grief.

Service is the key to success.

A Moment of Truth

————

"Maybe she won't find out," Greg said to Allen over the phone. "You really think I have to tell her?"

Greg knew what he was going to hear: *yes.*

"You gotta bite the bullet on this one, buddy," Allen said. "Don't get angry at your wife. Get honest. Then apologize."

Greg hung up the cell phone and focused on driving. He flashed back to the night he'd met Serena at a restaurant. He and his wife were having some problems then, but now they'd started going to counseling. They were working things out. He had broken it off with Serena months ago. It didn't mean much, their affair. But now Serena was going ballistic. She said she was going to tell Greg's wife.

Allen was right. It would be better if his wife, Marlyss, heard this from him.

Greg drove home, put the car in the garage. His hands were sweating. What was he going to do? Just open his mouth and blurt this out?

He walked into the kitchen. Marlyss kissed him on the cheek. He patted her tummy. She was five months pregnant.

His daughter ran up and squeezed his leg. "Hi, Daddy. I'm glad you're home."

He looked at his daughter, then his wife.

What had he been thinking of, being willing to risk losing all this?

"Honey," he said, "we need to talk."

There's a horrifying moment to go through when a consequence we've created becomes manifest. The air is filled with remorse and dread. It can be hard to open our mouths and talk. I've had those moments more than once. The hardest part is when I ask the question *Who caused this?* and realize the answer is *I did.*

There are times when we genuinely regret the things we've done. Other times we regret we got caught.

Some of us may use the game of cause and effect to get even with another person, to show them how we really feel. Sometimes we just make a mistake. Some people are out of control. If we're creating too many moments of dread and remorse, drama addiction— or another issue or addiction—may be an underlying cause contributing to all the effects.

We may have difficulty seeing the game of cause and effect taking place because of the temporal space between our choice and when the consequence occurs. But the moment we made that choice, we created the consequence, too. Don't kid yourself.

Those chickens are coming home to roost.

It's simple but not easy to say the hard stuff in life. Just open your mouth and, without doing any more damage, tell the truth.

———

Choosing to take responsibility for ourselves and
for the consequences our choices create looks like hard work,
but it really sets us free.

The Drive Wasn't What He Expected

———

Robert was driving home from work in his Subaru that evening. It was 5:35. He pushed the tuner on the radio a couple of times, trying to find a song he liked. He couldn't, so he turned the radio off and popped in a favorite cassette.

He sang along to "How Great Thou Art" at the top of his voice. It was one of the many moments he'd had during the past year of feeling blessed by God.

After his divorce ten years ago, he thought he'd never be happy again. He hoped and dreamed that someday he could find someone to love, someone who loved him and wanted to stand by his side. Then Rosemary had come into his life.

His dreams had come true.

He had heard people talk about problems with blending families. He hadn't had any. He loved her three children as much as if they were his own. They loved him. Everything happened like people had told him it would: if you trust God and do the right thing, everything works out for the good.

He turned the corner onto the street where he lived, slowly approaching his driveway. It was fall. Most of the leaves were off the trees. It was cold outside but toasty warm in the car.

The moment Robert remembers most isn't the moment after; it's the moment before.

He couldn't pull into the driveway. It was full of stuff. What was all that stuff anyway? He looked closer. It was his. All his clothing and belongings were thrown into a heap.

Robert raced to the door. Pounded. Rosemary opened the door, looking just like she had every day for the past year except for the way she looked at him.

"Go away. It's over. Get out. We're through. I don't want to be married to you anymore."

Robert got his own apartment, but all he could say was *Why, why, why?* Robert's friends kept telling him there was a reason this happened, but he didn't know what it was. He kept seeing the scene in his head—whether he was at work or lying in bed at night. *Pull up in my driveway thinking everything's fine. All my stuff piled in a heap.* He didn't drink. He didn't smoke. He was attentive. He was a good husband and father.

"I don't understand it," he told his friends. "I can't figure out what caused that."

Rosemary wouldn't accept his calls. But his stepson called him at work.

"I miss you," his stepson said. "Why did you leave? Are you ever coming home?"

"I hope so," Robert said.

It was when his wife started seeing another man that Robert's friend Jack told him the two little rules that helped Robert survive.

"Don't do anything stupid," Jack said. "Don't do anything to hurt anyone else, and don't hurt yourself."

"But we were so much in love," Robert said. "She held me, told me how much I meant to her, said she'd never felt this way before."

"I said it before and I'll say it again," Jack said. "Maybe this time it'll be more than wind whipping past your ears. Rosemary is manic-depressive. This is her issue. It's not your fault."

Robert went to a therapist. He went to church and he prayed. About the time Robert started to let go, Rosemary finally called him.

"You're right and I'm wrong," his wife said. "I love you. I'm sorry. I'll go to therapy. Please come home."

Since the day Robert found his clothes in a pile, he had obsessed and fantasized about hearing those words. He hurried home to his wife, but it didn't take him long to realize that just coming home wasn't enough.

The driveway scene continued to play in his mind. The pain of separation was ended, but the pain wasn't gone. As hard as he tried, he couldn't pretend that what happened never took place.

If she did it to me once, she might do it again, he thought every day. *Things just aren't the same.*

What Robert really wanted was something nobody could give him: he wanted his life back the way it was before that one moment in time.

I was driving down a scenic route with a friend one day when my friend asked me to pull to the side of the road so he could take a photograph. The sign said No Stopping. *Hmm,* I thought. *I'll just keep the car in drive and let him take a quick snapshot.* I no sooner thought this than a highway patrolman appeared at my window. I rolled down the window.

"What's the problem, lady?" he asked. "Did you not see the sign, or did you choose to ignore it?"

In typical fashion I refused to give a straight answer and talked around his question, explaining that the car wasn't in park and I was on my way. The truthful answer was: I had chosen to ignore the sign and hoped I wouldn't get caught.

It's something I'd done before.

Back in my codependent days I liked to pretend that if I wished hard enough I could wish reality away. I had seen all the signs in my relationship—at least enough that now I'd run. I wanted the relationship based on my fantasy of who I wanted this man to be, not who he actually was. By God, I wanted it to work. I was convinced it was *God's will.*

I had waited and prayed, done the right thing. Wasn't this my reward? My trip to reality started with obsessively, like Robert, asking why. My question was really a substitute for saying how much I hurt.

There were some tough days and nights on the way.

It's painful when someone we love has a problem. It hurts when we lose our dreams. But rarely have I seen a person, even the most profoundly spiritual person, get a chunk of happily-ever-after as a reward from God.

Relationships are hard work. Some of them work out; some don't.

Didn't you see the sign?

———

Awareness is a choice.

Karma with Feet

Sally was leaving church when Kevin pulled her aside. "Have you heard?" he asked. "Mark's back in town."

"Mark?" she said. She tried to act casual, but just hearing his name made her feel more alive. That man—that angel, that monster, that karma with feet—was the love of her life. They had been together several times over the years. Each time it was a disaster. But each time when she'd run into him again after a separation, a tiny voice in her head would chime, "Maybe this time we could make it work."

"What's he up to?" Sally asked, forcing herself to speak slowly. "Is he living here again or just in town visiting for a while?"

Sally bit her lip, praying she'd get the information she needed without having to ask any more. In a matter of seconds, it was like God himself answered her prayer. She had the hotel name and location where Mark was staying. While her friend was still chattering at her, Sally was already figuring out how she could run into Mark.

I could call him. Or I could go sit in the lobby and read magazines, waiting for him to leave. It wouldn't be stalking. More like strategically placing myself.

Sally drove home, entered her apartment, and then paced the floor.

For some reason she didn't understand, it always felt like she had compelling unfinished business with Mark.

That's because you haven't let go, the quiet voice of reason said. *You keep hoping and praying he'll be someone he's not. It's Darth Vader without the mask whispering, "I'm your father, Luke—your father reincarnate"—and you're trying to make him well. He's not.*

Shut up, she whispered back to subdue this sane voice within. *You don't understand. We've been doing this dance for so many years. It's true love. The real thing.*

The length of time you've been doing the same stupid thing doesn't measure depth of love, the voice of reason replied. *It just means it's taken you a long time to learn.*

Sally stared at the phone. Stared at the car keys. Then instead of calling Mark or driving to his hotel, she sat down at her desk, opened a drawer, and pulled out a letter. It was one she had written to herself.

Dear Sally:

I'm writing this letter because I care about you, I really do. And every time you get involved with Mark, it hurts you and it hurts him.

Remember what happened last time? The fighting, the crying, the insanity that went on for weeks and months? I want you to really remember how it felt to be with him instead of walking down a selective vision memory lane.

What you experience when you think of Mark aren't your true memories. It's euphoric recall. It's not real.

I know if you're reading this you're probably feeling excited to see him again. Each time you think that if you do something better or different, you can make it work. You can't. Instead, each time the arguing and insanity gets worse. Chances are pretty good that if the same thing happens 100 times, it'll happen again the 101st—no matter how much time has elapsed.

Please take a moment before you see him. Feel what you really feel, instead of just feeling excited to see him again. He tells lies, but he tells them so well he believes them and so do you. He tortures you for your past. He plays with your mind. He makes you feel crazy and afraid.

You've worked hard to get where you are. Do you really want to trade your peace for another roller-coaster ride with him?

It's okay to let go of your fantasies and really let go of the past.

He loved you the best that he could. Now it's time to pick up the slack. This time, please love yourself.

Whew, that was a close one, Sally thought later, looking back on that day. She felt good. It had taken a while, but she'd finally learned she could change her future by catching herself right before that moment in time and choosing what she wanted to create.

I put the crock on the stove burner, turned the flame on low. *Gee, I hope that pot doesn't crack,* I thought. I simmered the meatballs and marinara sauce all afternoon while I worked. *So far, so good,* I thought toward the end of the day. *Just a little longer. They'll be done. I can eat.*

I frowned.

Hope that pot doesn't break, I thought again.

Half an hour later I was on the phone. I heard a big pop. The pot cracked. Split right in two.

"I knew that was going to happen," I said to my friend on the phone.

"No, you didn't know it," he said. "If you knew it, you wouldn't have had to learn."

It's not what others tell us we *should* know that matters. It's the lessons we get under our belts that count. When we don't *have* to go there anymore, we won't. Until then, it's not over yet.

Some people call that *learning the hard way.*

Cause-effect, cause-effect, cause-effect. Wham. The lights come on. I get it. Life isn't torturing me. I created this myself.

Congratulations. You passed the class. Let's see what's next.

It's easy to slide by the little choices so fast we're not even aware that we choose. Slow down. Breathe. Take an extra moment.

———

Choose to stay present for each step.

6

She Had to Explain

She looked in his eyes and spoke slowly. It was the clearest Erica had felt for a long time.

"This isn't about you," Erica said. "This is my fault. You didn't do anything wrong. I can't take care of myself and I don't know how to love you. I'm all screwed up on alcohol and drugs.

"You deserve better than me."

The nurse walked into the room. "It's time, Erica. You shouldn't have seen your baby. It's just going to make it harder."

Erica handed her son to the nurse. She looked away as they walked out the door. What had helped her through her months of pregnancy was knowing that for once in her life she was thinking about what was best for somebody else.

She hadn't prayed for a long time. She didn't know if God could hear. "Please take care of my baby," she said. "Whenever he thinks of me, tell him I didn't place him for adoption because he wasn't loved. Tell him it's the most loving thing I've ever done."

● ● ●

"How would you rate your pain," the doctor asked me when I was in getting some tests done on my heart.

"On a scale of one to ten?" I asked.

He said yes.

I made a quick objective analysis of where I was. "That's easy," I said. "This is only a two."

I watched the picture slowly form on the video monitor screen. It pumped and pulsed. This wasn't just a muscle, an internal organ. It's what all the spiritual philosophies talk about as being the essence of who we are, love, the spiritual path. This was a heart. Not just any heart. It was *mine*.

"Geez, it's a miracle that thing still works," I said.

Secretly, I was in awe.

They're confusing. They hurt. They stretch the muscle to the limit. We have to do our own bypass sometimes, making the choices known as *hard calls*. People tell us to go with the flow. But those hard calls usually require doing the opposite of what we feel and what we want, because we're taking the time to look at the big picture instead.

They're turning points, junctures in our lives and often in the lives of other people, too. Sometimes they're little. Sometimes they're huge. Only we know how to rate them on the pain scale of one to ten.

Hard calls turn our hearts from an ordinary muscle into the spirit of God.

Find yourself in a murky circumstance? In over your head? Keep screaming down a deadly path by using alcohol, or ask for help? Stay married, or leave? Let go of someone, or keep holding on? Do something you know isn't right, or do the right thing instead? Forgive, or keep resenting? Keep going, or quit?

When one option isn't acceptable and the other isn't preferred, grapple, struggle, pray. Muster up energy. Get as clear as you can be on what you're doing and why. Explain if you must. Then go ahead and make that choice.

You can look away if you need to, like Erica did. Sometimes hard calls hurt too much to watch at the time. They feel better later, not now.

Feelings are important. Feel them. Get them out. But acting on pure intentions—however tiny that pure part is—is the best and most powerful use possible of our gift of free will.

It's not just how we move mountains.

Purity is how we climb mountains and get to the top.

———

*In any situation we find ourselves in, it's never too late to stop
being an effect and become a cause for love.*

7

First Class

Marissa checked her e-mails. A lot of junk mail. One from a friend. Then her eyes lit up. My God. She actually heard from *him*.

She read the short note: *Loved meeting you on the plane. Can't wait to have lunch. Let me know what day is good for you. Jeremy.*

She time-traveled back to that day they met. She'd been visiting her folks. She was tired and crabby, waiting to see if she could even get a seat on the plane. Flying standby was inexpensive, but it had its downside, too.

Coach had been full. But the good news was she got to fly first-class.

She found her seat, settled in. The one seat on the plane that was still empty was the seat next to hers.

Great, she thought, resting back in the seat. *I was the last person to board. I get to sit alone. I can sleep all the way home.*

Then a man appeared standing next to her.

"Hate to bother you," he said. "But can I get in and sit down?"

She didn't pay much attention to him at first. It wasn't like her to chitchat with strangers on planes. She planned on sleeping on this flight; it was a long one. But she never slept. The two of them talked the entire time.

He was gorgeous. Those eyes. So gentle and deep. He was intelligent. Sensitive. He had read some of her favorite books. And that suit. It reeked of money and success. She loved powerful men.

The only problem was he was married. With kids.

She was surprised when he asked for a date. "I don't believe in dating married men," she had said.

"We don't have to make a big deal out of it. I like your company. We can just meet for lunch," he replied.

Marissa thought about it. What she did next surprised even her: "Here's my e-mail address. Get in touch with me if you'd like."

She paused. Then smiled. "I can always say no."

She didn't think she'd hear from him. And not this soon. She read the e-mail a couple of times, then picked up the telephone receiver and called her best friend. She told her all about him: handsome, successful, sensitive, and married with kids.

"Hold on," Marissa said when her friend started hollering. "That's why I didn't give him my phone number. I told him I thought it was wrong."

"It is," her friend replied. "And I'm not willing to put up with you when you get all crazy and guilty because you've violated your standards."

"But we're only talking about lunch," Marissa said. "What's the harm in that?"

"Tell me all about it, then," her friend said. "Go ahead. Project. Tell me exactly what's going to happen at lunch. Think ahead, Marissa. Tell me what's going to take place."

"We'll meet at the restaurant. Probably some quiet place."

"What are you going to order? Spaghetti and meatballs?"

Marissa thought about it. "I probably won't order much. Something easy to eat."

"Why?" her friend asked.

"Because it's embarrassing to chow down in front of a man."

"Not if he's just a friend," her friend said. "So what happens next?"

"We'll talk for a while, then go out to the parking lot."

"Then what?" Her friend said.

The whole picture became clear. It ran through Marissa's mind. She didn't have to say any more. It wasn't about lunch. The date was about sex. That handsome, gorgeous hunk with the sensitive eyes was really the devil wearing an Armani suit.

"Thanks," Marissa said.

"No problem," her friend said.

Marissa walked over to the computer, deleted the e-mail, and blocked any more messages coming from that address. What helped Marissa was a good friend who was willing to play truth or consequence.

Cause and effect is a game of ironies.

To keep it—whatever *it* is—we've got to give it away. To walk through the door, we need to hold it open for others and let them walk through first.

The real irony of learning to successfully—or as successfully as possible for human beings—play the game is a secret I've spent most of my life trying to learn. In some situations, yes, do what feels right and do what you think. But the voice of reason and intuition often speaks much more softly than the voice that eggs us into drama addiction and troublemaking. You know that one. It likes to light matches and play with fire.

Besides the big hard calls we make, there's another kind, too. It's the little ones we face each day: do the right thing, or stir up the pot. Do the next thing, or sit and sulk. Relax and let go, or obsess. Pick up the phone, call someone, and be of service; or dwell on how stuck and miserable you feel. Feel, or go numb. Do something that feels gentle, nurturing, and nice, or sit and torture ourselves.

We have times when we genuinely don't know what to do next. Confusion runs rampant. But every so often we get this little troublemaking voice egging us on. Making the hard calls isn't just doing the opposite of what we think; often it's doing the opposite of what that troublemaking part of us suggests we do next.

People get bored. We can sit in the dark. Light matches and play with fire. Or we can use our free will to play the game of cause and effect by making the little hard calls that bring real light into life.

Stomp. Scream. Cry. Tell someone how it feels. Talk it out, reason it through first.

The hardest person to be honest with is usually ourselves.

He Hit the Wall

————

Jonathan had hit the wall.

He wanted to put his fist through it. Instead, he had to pick up his paintbrush and paint it. He slapped the paint on, stewing and muttering to himself.

This house was a mansion. These people had more money than God. He had spent four years in college. Then he had worked for peanuts to develop a track record. He was good at what he did, too—architectural designing and business administration.

Could he get a job doing what he had trained for? No.

The only way he could feed himself was by painting rich people's bathrooms and kitchens and bedrooms—rooms that didn't need any more paint.

He poured some more paint into the paint tray, and then went back to the wall in front of him. He had finished edging. Now he was using the roller. This didn't give him any satisfaction. It wasn't fulfilling. Busywork. That's all it was. What was wrong that he couldn't get his career, his dream, off the ground? These people had everything in the world, and he was stuck in their bathroom with a can of stinking paint.

"If you surrender to God's will, things will flow easy."

That's what everyone had told him for years.

He prayed and meditated every day. Sometimes twice a day. And it wasn't easy. Wasn't even close. For over a year now, he just kept hitting walls.

"If you do the right thing, good things will happen to you."

He wanted to do AIDS housing. What could be more right than that?

He wasn't just upset that he couldn't get his job. He was angry with God. And every day it was getting harder to believe in what he'd been taught. What was a guy supposed to do when he followed the rules, and what he thought were the rules weren't really the rules after all?

Jonathan didn't know what was coming next. He didn't know what to do. All he could see was what was right in front of him: another wall. The only thing that helped him was painting the wall in front of him and telling a few friends how disappointed he was in God.

Three years from that day, he would describe the situation differently. Jonathan would say how frustrated he was when he had to paint walls and see everyone else living their dreams when he barely had any faith left at all.

Then he'd say how much that emotional experience helped him to work with the people he was providing housing for because many of them felt the same way—only at a much deeper level. He'd talk about sometimes needing training that went beyond what you could get in school or in an office—and that not knowing what was taking place, not even understanding the experience, was important and necessary because if you knew, you wouldn't immerse yourself in the experience. You'd just wait. You wouldn't learn.

He'd tell you how well the rules worked. Then he'd explain that surrendering to God's will meant that sometimes you hit a wall but that the wall wasn't really a wall after all.

So if we do good things, good things will happen? And if we make negative choices, negative consequences will occur? If cause and effect is the name of the game, are those the rules? Remember Sherry, the pregnant woman who got in the car with someone she didn't know had been using drugs? What about her daughter? What were they doing wrong? And what about when we think we're making the right choice and it backfires, doesn't work, or turns out wrong?

Each time I jump out of an airplane I know I'm going down, not up. The law of gravity always works.

So does the law of cause and effect.

———————

When we do A and we hit the wall because it doesn't
lead to B—or at least not the B that we thought and planned—
it's not that the rules or the law don't work.
That's when the real game begins.

LIVING IN THE MYSTERY

Steeplechase.

I woke up in the middle of the night one night, startled out of a deep sleep, saying that word out loud. It had been said—*yelled*—to me in the dream.

For weeks I wondered what it meant, and why the word had been spoken so loudly. I looked it up in the dictionary: "A race across open country or an obstacle course"? I couldn't figure it out.

It's probably someone's name, I thought.

I was in the midst of trying to make sense out of a trip I had already taken to China and Tibet, where I had climbed the steps to four holy mountains. I was planning to return to Tibet to visit Mount Kailash, known to many Buddhists as the holiest mountain there. That's when the thought occurred almost as loudly as the original word.

It's not someone's name. It's the name of the game.

It started by being frustrated and climbing into a cave.

"I'm not going in there," I said, looking at the small opening between the rocks. "It's a dirty, dark cave."

I had come to China because I wanted to visit Tibet. To get visas and permits for Tibet, it was best to go to China first to expedite doing that. Then my friend Joe and I decided to climb the four holy mountains in China first, as long as we were here. *Who knows if we'll ever be here again?* I wasn't sure why I agreed, but it felt right at the time.

Now we were standing outside a cave by the sea in Putuoshan, a small Chinese island that was the home of holy mountain number one.

I was looking for magic and mystery, but the harder I tried to find it, the more ordinary everything became. People had pointed and stared since I got on the train in Hong Kong. Chinese people kept trying to convince me to eat fish heads and eel. Nobody spoke English except to point at me, giggle, and mockingly say *hello*. Spitting was a popular thing.

The ferry ride from Shanghai to Putuoshan had been long and loud. Music had screeched and blared from the boat's karaoke bar all night. I closed the window, but it got too hot. Then a flatulating man decided to sleep on the deck right outside the open window to my room.

My left knee was swollen to the size of a small cantaloupe from the sixty-pound pack strapped to my back. I wasn't really walking. More like *tottering along*.

And I hadn't even climbed the first mountain yet.

"Just come on in," Joe said. "We're here. Let's look around."

I climbed through the small opening. It looked ordinary enough. Light filtered in through cracks in the rocks in the wall. Puddles on the floor. A little trash. That funny cavelike smell: earth and age.

Next to the exterior wall were a small wooden table and a broken chair. I wondered if a monk had sat and meditated there. I wondered what he thought while sitting in this room. A little stone doorway led to another room. I peeked in. Eight inches of water on the floor.

In the other direction, all I could see was blackness. I didn't know if there was a wall or if the blackness actually led somewhere.

"Want to check it out?" Joe asked.

"Why not?" I said.

The blackness was all around me. No light left. I couldn't see. I didn't know what was under my feet. Didn't know what if anything was ahead. *Watch out*, I thought. *Be careful.* Heightened awareness kicked in. *Slow down. Breathe. Feel your way through. You know how to take care of yourself when you don't know what's next. You've been in that situation many times.*

"So what do I do now that I'm in recovery," I asked my chemical dependency counselor when I went to treatment in 1973. "Not that much," she replied. "Just change everything in your life."

By 1980 I was exhausted. Depleted. Worn out to the bone from trying to make an alcoholic stop drinking and love me the way I wanted to be loved. I had run out of ideas and run out of myself. "Why don't you learn a new way?" someone had suggested. "Let go of what you can't change, and begin focusing on taking care of yourself." I was dumbfounded. I didn't have a clue what it meant to stop controlling others and live my own life.

I stood in the parking lot outside the courtroom six years later. In one moment, I felt both exhilarated and terrified. I was free from a marriage that hadn't worked longer than it had. But I was also on my own—a single parent, raising two kids.

I sat in the hotel corridor. It was 1991 now. I couldn't remember which room was mine, or how to get there. I couldn't function, couldn't reason my way through. Faces and names had blurred at the funeral. I was in shock, in a daze. "Which casket do you want?" they had asked. "Don't you understand, don't you get it?" I said. "I don't want any of them. I want my son back. Alive." All my dreams, plans, hopes for the future—good dreams about being a mom, having two teenage children to love and care for, being able to support them and enjoy my work—everything had blown up in my face. It wasn't that I didn't know what to do next. I didn't know what to do now.

I stood at the door of the airplane. June 20, 1999. Ready. Set. "No!" I screamed. "It's 12,500 feet down. I could die!" "Your odds of dying in traffic on the freeway are a lot bigger. Yeah, you could die. But why don't you get out of the plane, because you could have a lot of fun, too."

In the cave, I fumbled through the darkness, carefully taking each step. Where was this leading? Anywhere? Finally I saw a glimmer of light. I stepped toward it. A wooden door led to the street.

That wasn't just a dirty, dark cave, I thought later. *That was the ancient cave of the unknown.*

There's more to life than we can see with our physical eyes. People have been talking about this for years. Richard Bach wrote about it when he introduced us to Jonathan Livingston Seagull, a bird that suspected there was more to life than what he saw, then used that insight to learn how to soar. Joseph Campbell told us what to expect. *The Hero's Journey,* it's called. We'd meet mentors and enemies and experience resistance as we journeyed into the innermost cave to find the gold. Then, once we had it clutched in our hands, we'd almost get killed on the long road home. Bill Wilson, in the *Big Book of Alcoholics Anonymous,* described it as being catapulted into the fourth dimension of existence. Margery Williams wrote a story about it for children, *The Velveteen Rabbit.*

She called this mysterious process *becoming real.*

I like mysteries. I like the concept of the Hero's Journey. I identify with Jonathan Livingston Seagull. *The Velveteen Rabbit* makes me weep.

And living in the fourth dimension that Bill describes makes life worthwhile. Like a friend said recently, "When I'm just living out of my head and not by intuition, life becomes ordinary, plain, ugh."

Although many of us are enamored with the idea of the mysterious process of growth and change described in *Jonathan Livingston Seagull* or *The Hero's Journey,* it's another issue entirely to find ourselves living through it in our lives—especially when change begins. We set our sights on a goal. We make a decision about how something is going to be. Then we plod forward. Wham. It isn't what we expected.

A didn't lead to our planned B.

Most of us like the concept of mysteries: reading them, watching them on TV. But we don't like living through the process and with a mystery of our own. It's not just that we want to know what's next; we don't understand what's happening right now.

Call it the void, the unknown—whatever you choose. But it's a place we go first, before we learn anything new. Fill up a glass with water. Right to the top. Now, try to pour some more water in. You can try—but you can't do it. You have to empty the glass first, before you can fill it with anything else.

It's a simple principle, easily overlooked.

There's a lot of power in an empty space.

We can't hold on to the old ways—the thoughts, the projections, the beliefs about how things have to be—and still be open to learning something new.

"Whether it comes in the form of curiosity, bewilderment, shock, or relaxation isn't really the issue," wrote Pema Chödrön in *The Places That Scare You.* "We train when we're caught off guard and when our life is up in the air."

Feel as frustrated as you want. It's better than staying numb. Try to control everything until you run out of yourself. Get depleted if you must. Then turn frustration into fascination. Gain control another way. Deliberately choose to enter the cave of the unknown.

Step carefully. It's okay if you can't see. It's better that way. Your other senses will kick in. Relax. Breathe. Feel your way through, until you see a glimmer of light.

The hardest thing to remember is that we're not in there alone.

"People like to choose the familiar over the unknown," a friend said one day, "even if what's familiar doesn't work and isn't what they like or want." In this section, we'll look at some stories about people who chose the unknown—or were chosen by it—and how that worked for them.

It's easy to stop outside the door to that cave and say, *I'm not going in there. It's dark. I'm tired and scared. Thank you anyway, I'll stay with what I can see and what I know.* Whether you're motivated by fear, curiosity, guilt, despair, or circumstance, my hope is that these stories will encourage you to take it one step further.

Let go of what you think you know.

Step inside. Look around. It's okay if you can't figure things out. Shhh. Listen to the secret: the more you're willing to surrender control, the more powerful you'll become.

Welcome to the mystery of life.

She Found the Key

Darlene was already in a foul mood the day her mother called—drunk.

Darlene's last marriage had been one more fatal attraction that quickly went bad. The only reason she had hung on for as long as she did was that he had a lot of what she needed: money.

The relationship she was in now was messy. Darlene did everything she knew to do her part. She was charming, witty, and beautiful. Attentive to his every need. And the harder she tried to pull him in, the further away he pulled.

It wasn't working. She didn't even know why she called it a *relationship*. The only relationship they had was in her mind.

It had been a lot to bear when her youngest brother had committed suicide six years ago. It had been a lot for her and her mother. But now this fluke twist of fate. Who would have thought a person could get that injured falling off utility steps in a kitchen? Her sister had been visiting her mother, helping her clean her kitchen. One moment she was on the ladder cleaning cupboards; the next she was lying on the floor.

It was too much when her mother called—drunk—with the doctor's most recent prognosis: her sister would be in a coma, para-lyzed, for the rest of her life. The swelling from the concussion had permanently damaged part of her brain.

Darlene called a friend. Her friend listened, and then shared some advice.

"The hardest thing for me was understanding that letting go didn't mean letting go of people, places, and things," Darlene's friend said. "It was letting go of my ideas about how life should go."

"That day my mother called drunk was my bottoming out," Darlene said. "All of it—the relationships, my mom's alcoholism, my brother's death, my sister's injury—became too much. Any illu-sions I had about being able to control life disappeared.

"I finally just surrendered.

"I let go."

Three years later, Darlene picked up the telephone and called her mom. It was the evening before Darlene's wedding. Who would have thought she'd be marrying a guy like this? She had turned him down when he first asked her for a date. "He's a nerd," she'd told her friends.

What she had learned over the next year was that this nerd was a good guy. He treated her well. And she no longer felt like she had to manipulate and control men to be taken care of because she could take care of herself.

"It became easier to take care of myself than to try to manipu-late everyone around me into taking care of me," she said. "It also set me free. I didn't have to be in a relationship for survival. I could be there for other reasons—friendship, play, and laughter. Love.

"I could be myself."

Darlene's mother answered the phone. She was tipsy, but not

slurring drunk. Darlene talked with her about her sister. Darlene tried to visit her in the nursing home at least once a week. There wasn't much she could do there. Darlene talked about how excited she was to be getting married. They were planning a small elopement ceremony, then a romantic honeymoon. Her mother said she was happy for her.

"I was just thinking about things," Darlene said, "and realizing how hard this must be for you, with Sis so sick, and all. How hard it must have been raising us kids alone, with no help from Dad. Remember when Uncle Terry came to live with us?"

Her mom said yes, she remembered.

"Well, remember how when I told you that he was touching me in bad ways, you didn't think twice about it? You believed me, and you just booted him right out?"

Her mom said yes, she remembered that, too.

"I'm just calling to thank you for that," Darlene said. "It meant a lot to me that you protected me and you cared."

Sometimes the unknown that we're called to enter is the entire journey of our lives. We start out with an idea about how life should go, and then we realize it's not going that way, but we keep hanging on to it because we don't know what else to do or think. Slowly, life wears away our resistance. And we still hold on because we can't imagine what to think or how to conceptualize what this journey is about. We can't imagine where it might go if it's not going where we imagined it would.

Stop thinking you know how life should go. Most likely, you don't.

It's not always a person or a thing we're letting go of. Sometimes letting go of our ideas about how things should be, how they should feel, and what's coming next is what we need to do to go into the unknown.

Going into the unknown isn't just something we do when things go wrong. The happiest people I know are people who wake up each day with an attitude of wonder and awe—or at least a willingness to stumble reluctantly into the unknown.

"I give myself a migraine every time I try to control life," a friend of mine said one day.

"I know," I said. "I've been known to make myself physically ill by trying to control things I can't."

Shed the illusions one by one. Complain. Gripe. Cry. Feel. Grieve.

There's nothing wrong with having hopes, plans, and dreams. But most of life doesn't work out exactly as we thought and hoped it would. Events have their own way of transpiring, unfolding, and taking place. Even the things that are good in life usually work out differently from what we thought.

Darlene found the key to her power when she surrendered to a big pile of pain. Not all people have as tough of a road as Darlene. Some have a lighter path; some have it worse.

Surrendering control doesn't mean relinquishing our power. It does the opposite. It gives us the power to quietly choose how we want to act.

———

*Letting go of our ideas about how life should go
is a choice that sets life's magic free.*

2

An Angel Whispered to Him

———

Aaron couldn't step into his future. He couldn't go back to his past. He looked around at his life. There wasn't much happening now.

Ten months ago, his wife had come home from work, looked him in the eye, and said she was divorcing him. Then she was gone.

Three months later, he lost his job. It wasn't the best job in the world, but it was his. Now it was summer in the Midwest. He didn't have a relationship. He didn't have a job. He didn't have any prospects. And his bank account was dwindling fast.

He didn't know what to do next. Hell, he didn't know what to do now.

He put on his bathing suit and jumped into the pool.

When am I going to be happy again? he wondered, doing laps. What he heard was a quiet thought, almost like it was whispered in his ear: *Why not be happy now?*

Two years later, Aaron would recall much differently that difficult time when he didn't understand what was happening. He would describe it as the beginning of a new cycle, a time when seeds were being planted for career and love that would blossom later. He'd tell you that the most important thing wasn't that eventually he got the money, the job, and a new girl. The most important thing Aaron learned was that it was okay to relax and sometimes even be happy when he didn't know what was going to happen next.

Of course we're not going to be happy all the time when we're wandering around in the dark. It's uncomfortable and frightening when we can't see the way ahead and don't know what's going on now.

There are many times I've felt forsaken by God, lacking intuition, without a clue about what to do next. Nothing I tried worked. And the harder I tried, the less right anything felt and the more fearful and paralyzed I'd become.

When I began skydiving I used to complain to my instructor about the wind. "Be grateful for the wind," he'd say. "You need it to push against. It's how you move your body around in the air. That's what it's there for—to help you fly."

Step into the blackness. Even the fear is an important part. At least we're feeling afraid; at least we're waking up. In skydiving, the air is what we need to push against. In life, it's often our confusion and fear.

Sometimes we need to take action—push against the resistance we're feeling. Sometimes the external pressure is quietly shaping and forming us into what we're about to become. Those times of not feeling guided, not feeling led, not knowing what to do next can be as powerful as taking clear action.

When we think we're alone, when we're frightened, it's our head talking, not our hearts. Stop trying to figure out the whole picture. You can't see it if it hasn't been shown to you yet. Trying to do the impossible will only make things worse.

Instead, focus on one little thing that's possible. Take a bath.

Take a shower. Jump into the pool and go for a swim. Get out of your head and calm those frazzled nerves. If you can't make it better—whatever it is—at least you can help yourself settle down and relax.

Life's magic—call it whatever you will—isn't a force we grasp for. We're naturally connected to the flow of things. When we just do the next possible thing—whether or not it's connected to solving the problem—life's magic comes to us.

———

When we're surrounded by things that look impossible,
making a simple choice to do something that's possible
is a powerful thing to do.

3

She Couldn't Decide

———

Jen rolled over in bed, as far away from him as she could. They had barely touched each other in months. The relationship was definitely on the rocks. He didn't think it was. He said he'd be happy to live this way the rest of his life. And she knew he would.

But was it what she wanted?

She honestly didn't know.

Security was nice. She could count on exactly what would happen each day. But security was beginning to feel more and more like a trap.

They didn't have children together. There was no important reason she could see to stay with him. But he didn't abuse or hurt her. The relationship wasn't dysfunctional. There was no pressing reason to leave.

She knew she wasn't in love, but she thought that was probably good. What had a friend told her long ago? *Never be in a relationship with anyone you're in love with. That will only guarantee pain.*

Whenever she thought about leaving him, she felt sad. And

scared. It might not be exactly what she wanted, but they were friends. They had shared some good times together. And at least she wasn't alone.

Jen made the best choice she could at the time.

"We'd been together for a year and a half. A year of it was good. For six months the relationship hadn't worked for me. I decided in fairness to him and me to give it six more months. It was hard to consciously live with how I felt, not knowing how things would go. It was even more frightening coming alive and recognizing I had needs and desires that weren't being met.

"It scared me to want anything—especially to want something I didn't have and didn't know if I could get."

Sometimes the unknown place we're called to enter
is what we don't yet know about ourselves.

4

He Saw the Light

———

John stared at the heart monitor, listening to it beep. The doctors said they had lost him for a few minutes.

John didn't feel as lost as he did before, though.

He had seen the light.

Alone in his hospital room, John stared at the phone, wondering if it was fair to call Monica now. From what the doctors said, he might have only five years left to live. He hadn't meant to hurt Monica when he refused to commit.

After eighteen years of marriage, working hard to support his wife, she had filed for divorce. "I need to find myself," she had said. "Besides, all you do is work."

He had asked her, "Is this what you really want?"

When she said yes, he just left.

He kept smiling, being people's best friend. But it had really hurt.

He met Monica after a couple of years. She was sweet, unassuming, patient, kind. But he knew she wanted more from him than he was able to give. She had put up with him for a while, given him a long string. Finally she had set him down. "You either com-mit to me, or I'm gone," she said.

Well, it wasn't the first time he had been left. Better to get the pain over with now. At least it gave him some control.

He tried to sit up. The monitor started beeping more loudly. He lay back down. Picked up the phone. The hardest thing to admit was that he needed Monica in his life. He told her what happened—that he had had a heart attack. Monica came to visit. He said he wanted to see her again. This time he was ready to commit.

She looked at him. He looked at her.

"I don't believe you," she said. "You're just being needy because you're sick."

A few weeks later, John got out of the hospital. He made a few changes in his diet, then started calling Monica again. She said she appreciated his calls, was glad he was feeling better, but now she wasn't willing to be hurt again.

John rang her doorbell the following week. He handed her the gift box. She opened it. Looked at what was inside. A diamond ring.

"I love you," John said. "Please . . . let's give us a chance."

They were married two months later in a quiet ceremony. Monica had flowers in her hair; John wore a new suit. She cried when they said, "I do."

John's days became filled with life and love. He and Monica took vacations. Sometimes they sat home and watched television—did the ordinary things.

The doctor was wrong. John didn't have five years. He was given three.

He died suddenly, while Monica was in the kitchen fixing din-ner one night. Monica walked into the living room to tell John it was time to eat. He was gone.

"His near-death experience made him a different man," Monica said. "All the little things that used to upset and irritate him so much didn't bother him anymore. We were so happy. But it was worth it—even though losing him really hurts."

John isn't around to finish his story, but he'd probably say that going into the unknown and choosing to love—even though love could hurt him—was a good call. Seeing the light made him realize that not loving could hurt him more than loving ever could.

It caught me off guard and by surprise. I was visiting my mother, sitting at her kitchen table, looking at a stack of photos. One of the pictures was of my grandson Julian, my daughter Nichole's first child.

I looked at the picture. My heart flooded with something.

Oh my God, I thought. *When did that happen? I let my guard down. Someone's gotten in again.*

The feeling I felt was love.

Oh, the things we do to protect ourselves and gain a sense of control. Do you know how brave you've been to get through everything you've endured? Many of us have had to shut down at such a deep level just to survive.

Coping with all the losses life throws at us takes a lot of skill.

Don't trust anyone. Don't be vulnerable. If you do you'll be disappointed. You'll only be hurt. Play it safe. Stay in control.

Some of us may have protected ourselves a little bit too much.

"Melody, you're so brave when it comes to things like jumping out of airplanes or pounding around foreign countries. Why are you so frightened of being open and vulnerable to another human being?" a friend asked one day.

I thought about the question. Probably because the worst that can happen when I risk jumping out of a plane is breaking my body, but what can happen to me when I open to another person is getting my heart broken. Again.

I learned the lesson early in life that nobody could make me happy or make me sad. The task of making me happy and finding fulfillment rested solely with me. But there's another side to that story. While love and relationships and other people aren't responsible for making us happy, the people we let into our lives can be part of our happiness.

Yes, some relationships are predictably disastrous from day one—at least when we look back at the whole ordeal. Many of our attempts at love just didn't work out the way we wanted and hoped. And some people are what we call addicted to love—falling in and out of love every other day. But don't let all this therapy jazz spoil some of the greatest joys in life.

A friend sent me a letter one day. It was written by a woman who had lost her son when he was fourteen. She was celebrating what would have been his twenty-second birthday by remembering and celebrating his life. She talked about how happy it had made her to see him skateboard, struggle through his problems, even argue with her about things. She talked about the pain and agony he went through as he experienced his first romantic relationship—something we call a teenage crush. She ended her letter this way: "What I'm happiest for is that the last year of his life he got to experience falling in love."

Maybe you could let your guard down, just a little. If it's really hard to do, maybe ask God to take your hand and help you. Letting people in and being vulnerable enough to let someone in—whether it's romantic, with family or friends—is risky business, but it's our choice.

Yes, it's important to love ourselves. But come on. Doing only that gets boring after a while.

———

Take a risk. Let yourself love someone else.

5

She Stopped Running

———

Jamie awoke at sunrise, made a pot of coffee, went outside, and grabbed the newspaper. She still didn't know why he had to confess.

Five years she had been with this man. As he had stood there talking to her, telling her so much more than she needed or wanted to know about what he had done, all she could think of was *Shut up, stop talking, don't tell me this, your behavior disgusts me.*

She had told him that later. After she spent one week on tranquilizers, staying numb.

This relationship had seemed so different from her others. He seemed so nice. For God's sake, she had met him in church. Her usual pattern would have been to run—pack up his things and boot him out the door. For some reason, she didn't. She wasn't sleeping with him. She had moved into the other bedroom. Demanded that he get into therapy. But a part of her was curious. *Why is this happening? Is there something I can learn about myself?*

She hadn't gone to therapy. But some things began to unravel. Her dad's funeral when she was five. Her mother had popped a tranquilizer into Jamie's mouth: "Here, it'll make you feel better, honey. No reason for you to feel pain."

She didn't stay because she was afraid to be alone or because she needed his money. She had her own career. Her own life. Her own hobbies. She was an independent woman, to the max.

She stayed because for the first time in her life she wanted to see this thing through instead of leaving with unfinished business. And for the first time, she trusted herself to know when it was done.

Since her decision to stay, little pieces of information had been coming to her that helped her do the next thing—the right people, at the right time, saying just what she needed to hear.

It felt to Jamie like living this way—letting things unfold and trusting that it would be okay—was what some of her friends called *letting go and letting God* and surrendering *your will.*

She had gone on-line after the *incident.* Met people on the Internet who had dealt with similar problems and were helping her heal. She had met a woman on-line who ran a bulletin board. It's funny. Just yesterday she had heard the strangest thought.

You're going to meet this woman soon. She'll be coming to town.

Later, when she stopped at the convenience store at the gas station, her attention had been drawn to the candy counter. It was the stupidest thing, but a box of candy jumped out at her. One of the letters on the packaging was missing. It should have read *Melody's Pops* but it didn't.

All it said was *Melody's Pop.*

Jamie scanned the newspaper, drinking her coffee. For some odd reason, she found herself drawn to the obituaries. She never read them. Wasn't interested. Today, she couldn't stop. One in particular drew her attention. She didn't recognize the first or last name of the man who had died, but she read the obituary all the way through anyway. My God, Jamie thought. Melody Beattie's on the road doing speaking engagements. Her father just died.

● ● ●

I was in a hotel room in Washington, D.C. It was a hectic time to travel—just shortly after the tragedy of September 11, 2001, when the World Trade Center was attacked. I was tired. My schedule was intense on the road. "Keep me busy if you're going to take me away from home," I had said.

As often happens, the people sponsoring me in town had arranged for my hotel room but hadn't turned on the long-distance phone service in my room. They were just protecting themselves against a potential author who might get bored and have a case of long-distance telephonitis all night. I couldn't call out. I hadn't told anyone my itinerary. I hadn't known until the day before I left California exactly where I was going to be. It happens sometimes when you're touring. I had learned for the most part to go with the flow.

I hadn't brought my cell phone with me, either—so no one could call me and I couldn't retrieve my messages. It hadn't been working right lately anyway. I had brought my laptop computer with me, though. I tried to go on-line that morning, check my e-mails. My server wasn't working right. It worked just long enough to let one e-mail through; then my on-line connection failed.

Hmm. It was from Jamie. I read it.

"Melody," she wrote. "I'm so sorry to hear about your loss."

My father had left home when I was three. Hadn't seen him much over the years. His family wasn't sure how to get in touch with me. They hoped if they put my name in the obituary, someone would let me know he had died.

I had just enough time to rearrange my schedule and, with so many flights being canceled and so many flights being full, make it back to my hometown in time for the funeral.

The memorial service was a quiet one. My stepbrother said a few words. "There's no denying that Dad had his issues," he said.

"But for today, let's remember the good that he did and the gifts his life brought to each one of us."

"When I first heard about ideas like surrendering your will to God, I thought that meant I'd have to go do missionary work in Africa, or something like that," Jamie said. "I didn't want to do that. It sounded awful to me. Then I realized that it meant something else, something even harder to do at first—standing still and being present for the experiences in my own life. Then letting these experiences unfold, trusting that a Greater Good was taking place, even when those experiences hurt.

"The funny thing is, now that I've experienced what it's like to surrender to a Higher Power, I wouldn't mind going to Africa. This spirituality thing is different than I thought. My family always told me to avoid pain at any costs. What I'm learning is that pain is really a present, a gift from the universe to help us look at life a new way."

When Jamie stopped running and entered the unknown, she ran into herself and God.

Sometimes life throws a brick at us just to get our attention. Heightened awareness is a choice too.

Trusting what we're learning—even when we don't understand it—is how life's mysteries are revealed.

6

She Saw a Monster in Her Bedroom

His snoring woke her up that day. Marge was barely aware of her own thoughts as she forced herself out of bed. They were the same thoughts she thought every day. *Does his worsening snoring mean his heart condition is getting worse? Will he die soon? How much longer do I have to wait to be free?* Getting up each morning was like pushing herself into a closet. It was dark. She didn't have much room to move.

She poured herself a cup of coffee and opened the newspaper. Soon he'd be coughing and hacking his way down to the kitchen. He'd either throw something across the room and break it . . . or he'd call her a nasty name.

If he woke up in a really foul mood, he'd do both.

She could run her day through her mind, and predict almost everything that would take place. He'd scream for lunch, supper too. If she talked too long on the phone, he'd yank the receiver out of her hand. She'd do some laundry, watch the clock. At eight o'clock, he'd have two drinks. Then he'd go to bed. She'd have three or four hours to do whatever she wanted. Sometimes she forced herself to stay up later, but she needed her sleep. Sleeping later than he did in the morning wasn't allowed.

It wasn't the life of her dreams. She couldn't even remember what her dreams were anymore. Husband. Children. Something about love. But at least this was predictable, and to her, predictable meant safe. She knew what to expect, and she was strong.

She could cope.

She was so used to the feeling, she didn't recognize it: dread.

There was no reason for this morning to be any different from all the others. Maybe it was bits from the talk show she watched every afternoon—well, when he allowed it—finally sinking in. A glimmer of a light came on. The print in the newspaper story she was reading blurred.

I'm not just waiting for him to die. I'm watching the clock tick until my death, too.

Marge grabbed the phone book, locked herself in the bathroom, and called for help. What she had seen this morning scared her. There was a monster in her bedroom. If she didn't do something quickly, she wouldn't get to have a life.

Later that week, when she was supposed to be out grocery shopping, she went for her first therapy session. The monster thought she was just dallying at the grocery store. Ha!

She started talking about feelings, her childhood, her life now—really getting things out into the light and the air. She began to understand that she didn't make him a monster—he was that way all by himself. And that if it made her unhappy, she could leave. Next she found a job. It didn't pay that well, but it paid enough. Then she bought a car. Then she rented her own place.

Slowly, each step into the unknown led to a new life. It felt strange and uncomfortable at first. Now Marge will tell you that if she can do it, anyone can. She was seventy-one the day she woke up, saw a monster in her bedroom, and stepped into the unknown.

I was talking to a group of people in Syracuse, New York, when a woman raised her hand. "Exactly what are the rules for taking care of yourself?" she asked. "I'm brand-new to this game, and I find myself fumbling around a lot."

I started to answer her—blah, blah, blah. Then I stopped myself short. She had almost hooked me.

Whether it's learning about codependency, recovering from chemical addiction, learning how to take care of children, learning to be married, or acquiring any new skill, being a newcomer is hard.

We watch others do with ease things we feel we'll never grasp or understand. People often have their own jargon—their own shortcuts for talking about what they're doing. Hearing this jargon can be like listening to a foreign language.

"I'll never get this," we think. "And I don't have a clue what those people are talking about."

As hard as it is to be a newcomer at anything, it's an important place to be. The very act of struggling through, not knowing, making mistakes, trying one thing, failing, getting frustrated, then trying another is how we learn. We're using muscles we've never used before—whether those muscles are physical, mental, spiritual, emotional—or a combination.

Like a new pony learning to stand and walk, we need time to develop muscle memory about whatever we're learning to do.

Ask questions; try to pick people's brains. They can give us bits and pieces. They can offer support, encouragement, and their opinion. Feedback, love, support, and training from a mentor or sponsor can be extraordinarily valuable. But there is no substitute for the awkward process of fumbling around in the dark while we learn how it feels to do something right.

It's possible to change our lives dramatically by a simple decision to at least be open to something new.

7

She Liked It

———

It was just a weekend, no big deal. But she found herself acutely alone.

It had been four or five months since Kelly ended her last relationship. She had been dating her boyfriend for a year and a half. She hadn't been terribly in love with him, but it had been safe. Predictable. She had someone by her side.

She had been dating a little since the breakup, but nothing had worked out well. She'd get herself all excited about dating, then quickly lose hope. Despite herself, she found herself turning down requests for dates. It wasn't that she was isolating. She had just learned too much over the past years.

Nobody in her life right now was what she wanted. And she was tired of clinging to someone just to avoid being alone.

Until this weekend, that is.

She stared at the phone, waiting for it to ring.

She pulled out her personal phone book. She had numbers she could call. A couple of the old boyfriends were still available, circling the block. Was that what she wanted? No, no, no. She could run through each one in her mind, tell herself exactly what would happen, how it would turn out.

I'm not a victim, she thought, watching Friday night drag on endlessly. *I have a choice.*

It was the oddest feeling, though. Nothing felt right to do. And although she might have had choices, she didn't know what they were.

She tried calling some friends to see if they wanted to come over, watch TV. Nobody was home. Or at least they weren't taking her calls.

Okay, she thought. *I'll watch a movie by myself.* And she did. But when she woke up Saturday, that empty feeling was still going on.

Why doesn't someone call me? she thought. *At least if an old boyfriend called and wanted to date me tonight, I could turn him down. Then I'd feel like I had a choice.*

The phone didn't ring.

The emptiness did ring—like a clanging bell. *Why didn't anything feel right? Why couldn't she get some sense of what to do?*

There was no reason for the awareness to set in when it did.

For years, I've been saying I want to go to the next level in my life. In my relationships. In love. But I never let go of the past long enough to go anywhere new, Kelly thought, staring at her quiet living room. *I always grab on to someone just to not be alone, to not be with myself.*

I hook up with people just to get a sense of where I'm going, because even though the relationship isn't what I want, it's familiar ground. I'm not alone, and I know what to expect—feeling bored and unhappy because I don't get what I want. I fill this empty space with anything just so I don't have to feel how empty it is.

The phone still didn't ring. She still didn't know what to do next. But Kelly relaxed. *No wonder this feels so strange,* she thought. *I am finally going to new territory. I'm in the void.*

I can't wait to see what unfolds, she thought Sunday night. *I'm learning something new.*

The cave of the unknown can be a dark and scary place. By choosing to say *I don't know*—at least to ourselves—we give permission for it to become a magical place, too. We don't always see the transformation while it's taking place. Only in retrospect do we see how powerful that time really was.

Some people will visit that cave only a few times in their lives. Others will visit it more often. Sometimes we step into it only because we have nowhere else to go. Other times, it creeps up on us. We just suddenly find ourselves there. Sometimes we think we're learning one thing, then we look back and realize that all along we were really developing other skills.

We usually don't know what we're learning while we're going through it. It can feel torturous, like a big mistake. Making a decision to consciously go into the unknown—even if we're kicking and screaming all the way—is how the transformation takes place.

We each have a different definition for stepping into the unknown at different times in our lives. It may be getting married, getting divorced, beginning a relationship, staying in a relationship to work out problems, or being willing to be alone. Making a decision to step into the unknown might be as simple as acknowledging that we don't know what to do next, then asking a friend, a therapist, or our Higher Power, God, for help.

We need to do as much as we can. But many people have discovered and live by this simple truth: God will do for us what we cannot do for ourselves. The magic lies somewhere in between.

The unknown can feel uncomfortable, frightening. There are no guarantees. But if it's all too familiar and comfortable, it's because we aren't doing anything new. Each lesson puts us in new territory, unfamiliar ground—the birth of a child, getting sick, a new career, starting life over after the children leave home, the death of a loved one, getting sober, tackling another kind of disorder such as OCD, ADD, or codependency issues.

Cultivate the sense of wonder that comes from not assuming, not projecting old beliefs on how life has to be. We don't have to have a problem, pain, or issue to walk into the void and experience the magic and mystery of life. We can do it each morning by waking up and living with humility, an open mind, and an open heart.

When you're not certain if there's ground under your feet, or where it leads, walk carefully. As surely as it's dark and frightening, there's magic there, too. When you're willing to let go of old ideas and frames of reference about how life is, has to be, always will be, and what's next, you're in the mysterious void, the place where all creation begins.

Walk slowly until you see the light, because you will. Then get ready. We've got a mountain to climb.

AS THE WHEEL TURNS

"Everyone likes to talk about karma," Joe said. "Nobody likes to talk about dharma—the lessons, and the opportunities to practice what we learn. And that old dharma wheel just keeps turning round and round, grinding us down like a piece of sand until we get it. Whatever *it* is."

It was 4:30 A.M. Time to put on the backpack and head toward holy mountain number one. Joe and I wound through the quiet streets on the small island, listening to Putuoshan waking up.

We walked past the Meditation Temple, next to the hotel. Then we turned left onto the path leading to the mountain.

I didn't know what to expect.

Mountain climbing wasn't my forte.

Soon, we began ascending concrete steps.

"This is it," Joe explained. "That's how you climb holy mountains in China. You walk up steps."

"How far is it to the top?" I asked.

"Don't start, Melody," Joe said. "We'll know when we're there because the stairway will end and the only direction the stairs will go is down."

The guidebook listed the peak on Putuoshan as three hundred meters in height. As I looked up and saw steps, steps, and more steps, the concept of meters didn't mean much to me. My knee hurt. I was tired of noodle bowl. I wanted toast. Butter. Eggs. Fat—American-style. But I was here, and despite the constant pain in my knee, determined to get to the top.

This was going to be the easiest of all the mountains to climb. The altitude was lower and so was the duration of the climb. I didn't understand a lot about altitude. I knew that the higher you got, the thinner the air. I understood that in places like Denver, where the altitude was high, I got a little woozy. I knew that when the airplane I skydived out of reached 12,500 feet, it was a little difficult to breathe. But I wasn't a mountain climber. I was on a spiritual quest.

Joe was the outdoorsman type—a self-labeled yuppie much younger than I—thirty-one years old—who was here to conquer the mountains and see the terrain. It was an unlikely combination, but we both hoped that our opposites would blend and create a good trip.

We climbed and climbed and climbed. It was like being caught on a gigantic Stairmaster, after a while. Some of the steps were narrow and steep; some were wide and the incline was small.

At first all I could think of was getting through the climb. If I made my left leg stiff and hauled it up each step, it hurt less. I pushed and pushed, getting more tired and out of breath with each stair.

Hurry to get through this. Hurry to get through that. Hurry to get to the top. Will I make it or not? Always one step ahead of myself, wondering where I was going next. *Slow down. Relax. Stay present for each step. It's not climbing the stairs that tires you. What tires you is pushing ahead out of urgency and fear and not being present for where you're at.*

Every step of the way there's something to learn. Fear. Guilt. Death. Loss. Relationships. Power. Money. Play. Forgiveness. Compassion. The lessons aren't incidental. In one of her books, Elisabeth Kübler-Ross called these lessons "The Wheel of Life."

Sometimes the lessons we learn are individual. It happens to one of us, but if we look around or study the statistics, it happens to many people during the course of their lives. The lesson changes our consciousness, but there are others who have been through similar experiences before us and others who will follow us down that path. We feel like we're going through it alone, but that's an illusion.

We're not.

Sometimes the lessons are more global in scale. An event or problem happens to a large enough group of people or to someone significant enough in a country that it affects mass consciousness simultaneously. We think, we feel, we search our values together, as individuals and as a group. And we don't have to look for others going through the lesson: they're all around us; they're right there.

Many of us have had lessons like codependency (learning to love and take care of ourselves), chemical dependency, or another addiction as part of the game. We've learned about service, about giving and receiving, and the importance of both. Other lessons that are universal are tolerance and faith.

Some of us have more lessons than others. The tricky part of these lessons is that when the winds blow a lesson our way, we can feel uncomfortable. We're not sure what's being worked out, and we'd prefer it if the wheel grinding us like a piece of sand stopped.

The concept of learning lessons during our lifetime isn't new. Remember Job from the Old Testament? A righteous man, he was called. Yet when he lost everything he had, his friends stood there pointing their fingers at him, saying, "Well, you must have done something awful to deserve this."

Job raged at God.

But when he finally learned the lessons—anger, acceptance, surrender, and, most important, forgiving his friends—that big grinding wheel turned.

On the mountain, once I slowed down, I began to feel a warm glow. Devotees postulated their way up the steps. Goats grazed on the hill. The shading from the bamboo forest made intricate designs on the steps. If I became thirsty, a spring would appear by the side of the road. If I became tired, I'd spot a place to rest.

Joe and I made it to the top of the steps. We visited the temple. Then we walked around the top of the mountain, visiting the little cubicles built into the side of the hill. Most of them were empty. In one of them, a monk sat meditating and praying. He nodded to us when we looked in, gesturing for us to enter.

We sat down.

He offered me a stick of incense to light and place on the altar. I did.

Being at the top of the mountain felt good—for a minute. But I still had to walk back down. On the way down I noticed that people had set up a shop by the spring by the side of the road. They were now selling the water that earlier was free. All our needs would be provided, but industrious people had managed to capitalize on that.

I laughed.

Slow down. Breathe. Make your choices. Take your chances. We don't escape experience. Take your place on the Wheel of Life.

"Hurry-worry never works," said Tsun Tsai in *Bones of the Master*. The magic isn't tomorrow or in some far-off place. The magic is in the moment and the exact details of the situation you're in right now.

The stories in this section will explore lessons people have gone through and choices they made that helped turn the wheel. Instead of asking *Why is this happening to me?* ask *Where am I, how do I feel, and what am I doing and learning right now?* The secret is being grateful for everything—every single thing—on the path, whether we *feel* thankful or not.

Night Shift

———

Marlene walked through the hospital doors and rode the elevator to the seventh floor. She hoped her shift would be quiet tonight. It was her first day back after three days off. Even though her patients were sick—some of them terminally ill—she liked it when they were peaceful and pain free.

She wound through the maze of hospital corridors until she reached her station. Arrrgh. Bonnie. At least Bonnie was leaving. She couldn't stand her. It irritated her just to check in with her.

Marlene bit her lip as Bonnie made her little comments about the status of the patients. "Number 212 is whining again. Always got something to complain about. You know how she is. Probably just a ploy for more pain meds. Number 209 sent all her food back from supper. Said it wasn't fit to eat. What does she think this is, room service at the Ritz?"

Marlene wanted to say, *They're not numbers, they have names.* By now, she was biting her lip so hard it hurt.

Just shut up, Marlene, she said to herself. *Don't cause a fight. She's your colleague, like it or not.*

"How's Mrs. Amison doing?" Marlene asked. Mrs. Amison was one of their patients that wasn't going to leave the hospital the same way she came in. She had a neurological disorder that was terminal. At best, she had another ten days to two weeks to live.

"Oh, Number 205? She's aspirating. She'll probably go tonight."

"What are you doing for her?" Marlene asked.

"She's in the final stages of dying. There's nothing to do," Bonnie said. "Just let her go."

Marlene looked around. Lorraine, the nursing assistant, had just arrived for her shift. "Can you help me for a while?" Marlene asked Lorraine.

Lorraine nodded.

"By the way, Number 205's been asking for you for the past few days," Bonnie said.

Marlene didn't look at her. "Thanks," she snapped.

One of these days I'm going to lose it with that woman, Marlene thought. *I'm going to blow up, lose control. Probably lose my job.*

Mrs. Amison's eyes lit up—just for a second—when she saw Marlene come into the room. Marlene gently straightened her bedcovers. She made sure Mrs. Amison's feet were covered and warm. She fixed the pillow under Mrs. Amison's head. She checked the IV, did some medical procedures. But mostly she sat there and held Mrs. Amison's hand.

Lorraine watched, helped, did as she was told as Marlene worked with Mrs. Amison. Mrs. Amison looked like she was in a lot of pain. What was different about Marlene from the other nurses was that Marlene wasn't afraid to look a dying patient in the eyes. And she wasn't afraid to be respectful and nice. Marlene treated dying people like real people every second they were alive.

Death still made Lorraine nervous. Sometimes it scared her a lot.

Mrs. Amison died within an hour after Marlene entered the room. Marlene sat with Mrs. Amison, sat right there with her, until the moment she died. It was almost like she was waiting for Marlene to say good-bye.

Or maybe, Marlene thought, *she just didn't want to go through it alone.*

Marlene didn't see anything extraordinary about herself. But both Lorraine and Mrs. Amison knew Marlene had a gift.

Marlene's father had died ten years ago. Marlene's thirteen-year-old daughter had committed suicide eight years ago. Marlene had found her, held her in her arms, been the one to call for the ambulance, even though it was already too late.

Why did you do this? she had wanted to scream. She hadn't. She just held her, then said good-bye.

Marlene never thought much about any good that had come from losing either her father or her daughter. She would have given anything in the world—anything—to have both of them alive and well. Marlene had been too busy surviving, doing the next thing, to notice the gift of compassion that had worked its way into her soul.

"This is going to be the most painful thing you've ever gone through. But good things will come out of it someday. I promise they will," my best friend, Echo, said to me following my son's death.

She was trying to give me a reason to keep going, but her words didn't cheer me. *Good might come out of this someday*, I thought. *But I'm not willing to pay the price.*

Some losses are so devastating that we will never be *happy* they happened. But it is possible to be happy again. Some events in life we can't control. And we'll make ourselves crazy if we try to look too diligently for the good that can come from a tragedy.

The gifts that come from any of our experiences don't have to be controlled, either. By staying present for every step, the gifts from each experience will emerge naturally, on their own. We may not notice or be grateful for good that's come from what we've lost, or the values some of our lessons have instilled in us—like compassion, tenderness, mercy, and love.

But other people will notice those gifts.

They'll be grateful we learned what we did.

Sometimes the best we can do is hunker down, protect ourselves, survive, and stumble through the really tough times. There were times when simply going to the grocery store took as much out of me as climbing a mountain did.

We don't have to accept all of life's realities in one moment. We don't have to get to a place where we totally accept losses that are too much to bear. We just need to focus on accepting each step. Each feeling (and there will be a lot of those). Each day. Each hour. Whatever it is we're doing right now. Slowly we'll begin to see that even that idea—being fully present for each moment and hour—is a practical and valuable way to live life.

First comes the trauma, the shock. Then the overwhelming grief. Then the numbed, stunned silent hours as we stare at the empty space left by what we've lost. Then the pain often becomes worse because we realize how much we've really lost. Then we trudge through the hours, going through the motions, trying to start moving again whether we want to or not. Then we try to be happy, even though we're not. Next everything we do has one focus—healing our pain so it's not so difficult to live life again. One day we wake up and find ourselves actually excited and engaged with our life, doing things we want, cohabiting with our loss. We're not happy about it, but to our surprise, we're at peace.

During the process that many call grief, we've learned to see things, people, life, and death in a new way. We'll never be the same again. But we weren't meant to be.

Life can be horrifying and holy in the same moment. And it is those horrifying moments that imperceptibly shape our lives.

Life and death. Cause and effect. None of us know how much time we have. "I don't like this whole impermanence thing," a friend said one day. "I'm not crazy about it either," I said. "But once you get the hang of it, you can work with it."

It's all the more reason to stay present for each step.

———

Grief isn't an abnormal condition. It's nature's way of healing our hearts. Choosing to face and heal from loss is one of the toughest calls we can make.

2

He Felt Spun

————

"Mom, I'm starting to flare again," Charlie said, racing out of his room.

His mother was on the telephone.

"Excuse me," she said to the person on the phone. "I've got to go."

Flare-up's weren't good. Charlie knew that. A couple of times ago when he flared, his mom had to call the cops. He was really angry, really upset. Then it occurred to him to break something— her favorite lamp. After he broke that, he broke something else. Once he started breaking things, he couldn't stop himself.

He didn't have to take off his belt, wrap it around himself, and pull on it like a lawnmower cord to get himself spinning like Joey Pigza did in *Joey Pigza Swallowed the Key*.

A lot of the time, Charlie felt like he was spinning in circles all on his own.

The medication helped him most of the time.

Now he was learning to catch his flare-ups. If he couldn't calm himself down by thinking the right thoughts, he was supposed to tell his mother or a responsible adult—like the teacher at his special school. Then they'd take him to a special place where he could stay for a couple days.

Charlie was learning to take responsibility for himself. It was easier to go to the special place and calm down than it was to go to kid's jail.

"I'm a special kid, huh, Mom," he said in the car as she drove him to the place where he'd go to calm down. Charlie's dad was gone. He drank too much. Charlie's brother had died. But Charlie didn't want to think about that. His mom was a good mom, but she had to work really, really hard.

For as long as Charlie could remember, he had just felt spun. The doctors said it was something called ADD. And decision impairment—those were the words they used—from some kind of injury to his brain.

"One more thing," Charlie said before she dropped him off.

"What's that, honey?" she asked.

"Do you think that when God gets bored, He just plays with us?"

Sometimes the lessons start way, way too soon. We have to start *learning* hard things at an early age. Some children and adults have ADD (attention deficit disorder). In most cases it's not as severe as Charlie's condition, which was complicated by an injury to the brain. But it can still interfere with learning, work, happiness, and achieving our daily goals. Some children and adults have a more difficult time with ADD, especially when that condition becomes complicated by some other disorder, including OCD (obsessive-compulsive disorder). Thank God help is available for most of the problems people have now—whether it's ADD, OCD, anxiety attacks, manic depression, or any number of other issues that interfere with our quality of health, choices, and life.

It might not feel fair or right that life has to be so hard. *But accepting the disorders that we or our children have—and finding the best solutions we can for them and ourselves—is a loving choice we can make.*

3

Her Room Was a Mess

———

Sally went into her daughter's room just to look around a bit.

The sheets and blankets were on the floor. Well, on what would have been the floor if you could see it under all the mess.

I'll just tidy up a bit, Sally thought, digging through some of the trash. "I knew it," she said out loud, picking a pad of rolling papers out of the mess. "She's using drugs again!"

Sally had already put her daughter in chemical-dependency treatment once. Things were great for about, oh, six weeks. A few weeks after Sally's daughter came home, she started getting mean and rude again. Blaming all her problems on Sally. Telling Sally that it was she—Sally—who needed to change.

"You're just all screwed up, Ma," her daughter said. "It's no wonder I use. Who wouldn't with a busybody snoop of a mother like you!"

This story's been told many times, but it bears repeating again. Eventually Sally's daughter went back to treatment. Eventually Sally went to Al-Anon.

The time in between?

"It was a living hell," Sally said.

Raising teenagers—with fluctuating hormones, vacillating between wanting independence and wanting to be children, just beginning to learn about the game of cause and effect—can challenge the patience of a saint.

Raising teenagers or children with chemical-dependency problems can be downright and impossibly hard.

It can be painful and confusing if we don't know they're using. We observe the changes in their behavior and wonder what went wrong. They can become surly, withdrawn, moody, evasive, and mean.

It hurts to watch children hurting themselves with alcohol and drugs, knowing that's what's taking place. It's frightening to think about all the possible consequences that could happen when they use. Problems with children can trigger so much guilt. I've heard stories covering the entire scale:

"I went to Al-Anon. My son went to treatment, he stopped using, it was a miracle, things were fine."

"I went to Al-Anon. My son didn't stop using for years, but I believe my changed attitude helped save his life."

"I went to Al-Anon. My son didn't stop using. He overdosed and died."

Then there's the classic tale: "I don't need help and neither does he. He's a good kid. Just a little messed up right now. But everything's fine."

It can be difficult to discern if a teenager is doing normal experimentation with alcohol and drugs or if there's a problem going on that needs assistance and help. Sometimes it's hard to know what to do and when. Two things about this are for sure. One is that if a child is potentially addicted to alcohol or drugs, that child stands a better chance of recovering from the problem if he or she gets professional help. Treatment may or may not take the first time, but at least the child knows that he or she *has* a problem—he or she isn't *the* problem—and there's a solution available to her or him. Seeds are planted that may sprout later on.

The second idea that's guaranteed is that if someone you love has a problem with alcohol or drugs, a good Al-Anon meeting for *you* helps.

———————

Taking our heads out of the sand is a good choice.
And no matter who has the problem that's driving us crazy,
it's our job and lesson to find our sanity and
take care of ourselves.

4

She Found Herself
in Nowhere

———

Jennifer sat across the breakfast table from her husband. She watched him eat his pancakes and eggs, smiled at him as he drank his orange juice. Like a record on the lowest level of volume, her thoughts played in the back of her mind. *I hate this town. I hate my life. And,* she thought, watching him pick up the newspaper, *I'm growing to hate him, too.*

This was the job of *his* dreams. He had studied for it, prepared for it. She had given up her friends, her life, to move to this small town in the middle of nowhere so he could be a microbiologist. He was content.

She was dying inside.

She had tried everything she knew not to feel the way she felt. She had gotten involved in volunteer work. She had tried to make friends. She had her job working in the accounting department for a local company. She had waited. She had prayed. Nothing, nothing she had done had worked.

And with all her heart, she didn't want to rain on his parade.

She loved him. She wanted to be married to him. She wanted to be his wife. At least she used to. Now the record of hating her life and hating him played continuously, each day.

There must be something wrong with me, Jennifer thought, cleaning up the kitchen and brushing his cheek with a good-bye kiss as he left for work. *Maybe if I try harder, I won't feel this way.*

Try what? a quiet voice said. *What's left to try? You've done everything you know to solve this problem. You hate your life more every day.*

I'll just endure, Jennifer thought. *I don't know what else to do.*

There was no apparent reason the phone should have rung that morning with a call from an old friend in the town where she used to live. Jennifer had tried to keep her old friendships vital, but as the days ground into months and time moved along, there had been less and less to talk about. When they asked her how she liked her new life, Jennifer would just lie and say, "It's fine."

There was no apparent reason Jennifer should have said anything differently that morning, should have said anything other than "I'm fine" when her friend asked how she was. It wasn't her style to be honest about how she felt—with anyone else, or herself. But in one gush, it came spewing out.

"Have you told your husband how you really feel?" her friend asked.

"Oh no," Jennifer said. "I couldn't do that."

"Honey, I think you need to take a look at your codependency," her friend finally said.

Jennifer had heard the word before. It applied to some people. Her old friend Marge, who was married to that beer-guzzling bum of a husband, Harry. Marge was codependent. Always chasing him around to bars, trying to make him stop drinking. Lying to his boss. Marge was a mess.

Jennifer wasn't codependent. She was, well, she was a good wife.

The literature and books came in the mail the following week. Her friend sent them to her, even though Jennifer said she didn't think the concept applied to her and her life. By the time they arrived in the mail, Jennifer had almost forgotten about the conversation they had.

Jennifer danced around the books for two weeks. She put them on the mantel, stared at them, then moved them to the desk in the den.

"What's that?" her husband asked.

"Oh nothing. Just some books my friend sent to me."

"Ummm," he said.

The books haunted Jennifer. Then she made a small choice: *She didn't have to label herself anything; but she could at least be open to reading the books*.

Jennifer read twenty pages and then threw the book she'd been reading across the room. Her fit of rage surprised even her. Especially her. Jennifer never, ever got mad. It wasn't who she was.

Then, before the book hit the floor, she started crying. And couldn't stop.

Nobody had ever told her what the book had said—that it was okay to be who she was. Nobody in her entire life. This subtle trying to make herself be someone else had permeated her since she was a child: trying to be a good student; trying to be a good daughter; trying to be a good wife. Somehow in trying so hard to be a good everything, she had disappeared. And she wasn't good at anything anymore, including living her own life.

The next months were the most frightening—and freeing—of her life.

It took her that long to work up the courage to tell her husband how she felt. Opening her mouth, being honest about who she was, even coming to believe that was okay, was the most unfamiliar place—even stranger than this town she was living in—she had visited in her life.

She had always prided herself on being so good and responsible. Now in her thirties, in a small town in the middle of nowhere, Jennifer was finally learning to surrender control and take responsibility for herself.

"While it was taking place, I felt so confused and lost," Jennifer later told a friend. "Now I look back on the whole experience, and it was the best thing that ever happened to me. I told my husband how I really felt. I told him I loved him and wanted to be his wife, that he could stay in this town if he wanted, but I had to take care of myself. He was shocked. But how could he have known before that? I had been pretending for so long, I didn't even know who I was anymore."

"We moved back to our hometown. Our marriage is stronger now than it was before. I wasn't a victim. I learned that. He hadn't done anything to me. I had done it to myself."

She calls her best friend on her cell phone from a bathroom stall at work after excusing herself from a board meeting and then bursting into tears. All she did was ask her boyfriend, described as a *vile, self-indulgent commitment phobic,* whom she's been seeing off and on for eighteen months, to take a vacation with her. He doesn't just decline the invitation; he breaks up with her on the spot.

Now she's trapped in the bathroom stall with dripping eyeliner and no makeup.

"I'm codependent," Jude says. "I asked for too much to satisfy my own neediness rather than need."

In the book, *Bridget Jones' Diary,* Bridget reports, *Typical, but Jude naturally was blaming it all on herself.*

In the movie, Bridget lovingly reassures Jude that she (Jude) isn't codependent; the now ex-boyfriend is a jerk.

"I read *Codependent No More,*" a woman TV host confessed after they ran a documentary-type spiel on my life. Her co-hosts looked at her. Was that horror I saw in their eyes? "That was back in my codependent days," the woman host quickly explained.

The first time I went to an Al-anon meeting, a perky woman met me at the door. "Welcome," she said. "You're an Al-anon." I didn't return the smile. "No, I'm not," I said. "I'm an alcoholic/addict." "Oh," she said, still smiling. Was that a glimmer of understanding I saw in her eyes? "You're a double winner. We're so glad you're here."

I wasn't. I was cringing with shame and madder than hell.

"Were you really one of *those?*" new friends ask me now.

I want to lie and say, *No I just worked with them. I was never like that.*

"Do you consider yourself codependent?" I asked a woman in her mid-twenties who obviously was.

"I prefer to think of myself as an over-carer instead," she said. "The thing is, when I care too much about one person, someone else doesn't get their fair share of my caring. And the person who goes without is usually me.

"Who wants to identify as an over-needy control freak? Not me," she said. "Identify yourself as a codependent privately, quietly. Then own your power loudly, so everyone can hear."

When I wrote *Codependent No More,* back in 1986, most people ascribed to the belief that it was our duty to control situations, attach ourselves to people, hang on, take responsibility for their behaviors, repress our emotions, feel guilty, and deprive and neglect ourselves. Somehow we had come to the societal and cultural conclusion that whatever was going on, behaving that way would help.

Now that common belief has changed. It is culturally and societally acceptable—even expected—that we take care of ourselves.

Over the years since I wrote *Codependent No More,* the collective feeling about codependents has become transformed from gratitude to the powers that be for isolating and naming that pain we call *codependency* to a reluctance to admit that we were or are one. We don't want to be associated with the word that symbolizes controlling, needless victimization and martyrdom, manipulation, and a regular routine of doormatting ourselves.

I don't like the *word* much myself.

But for the millions of people who have been intimately exposed to someone else's alcoholism or another similar disorder, codependency was and still is a life-saving word. As Jennifer discovered, recognizing, understanding, and dealing with *it* becomes a gateway to getting and keeping a life.

"When did you deal with your codependency?" I asked a woman one day.

"When I got tired of beating my head against a brick wall," she said, "trying to control everything and everyone except myself."

However we identify, being a victim is *out;* taking care of ourselves is *in.*

Self-care is finally a popular choice.

5

He Had to Backtrack

Doug swaggered down the corridor, following the man in the uniform. When the man stopped walking, Doug entered the jail cell. The door clanked shut behind him.

"Hey, Dougie!" someone yelled from down the hall. "What did they get you for this time?"

Doug walked to the door of his cell and looked around. It was his old buddy Carter. "Stealing a car," Doug said. "What are you in for?"

Later, the sheriff unlocked Doug's door and led him back through the maze of hallways. "Your dad's here," the sheriff said. He shook his head: "Doug, I've known your family for years. They're good people. Why are you doing this to them?"

Doug didn't answer. He followed the sheriff to the visiting area. There sat his dad.

Doug listened to his dad rave on: "Why are you doing this? How can you hurt your mother and me like this? After all we've done for you, you turn around and do this to us?"

Doug slumped in his chair, waiting for his dad to stop guilt-tripping him. Finally his dad stopped hollering. An uncomfortable silence filled the room. "My bail hearing's tomorrow morning," Doug said. "See you there."

His dad didn't yell now. He lowered his voice: "Your mom and I have turned ourselves inside out to help you, to give you another chance. It hasn't worked. You're back here again. And each time, your behavior gets worse.

"We called some people, your mom and I. We decided, well, we decided that we're not bailing you out this time. We've done everything we can. We're going to talk to the judge and ask that he sentence you to someplace that can do for you what we can't."

Doug watched his father stand up.

"I love you, Son," his father said. "But enough's enough."

Doug's father turned and walked to the door. The sheriff let him out. Then he came back for Doug. By now, the swagger had left Doug's step.

Six weeks later, Doug sat on the hard metal chair in the *group room*. What a joke this whole place was. He wished the judge had sent him to prison. At least they would have left him alone.

The counselor looked at Doug: "Sit up. Button your shirt. Take that cigarette out from behind your ear and throw it in the trash."

Doug sighed, then got up and walked to the wastebasket. The guy two seats over snickered at him. Doug made a fist and shot him a look.

"Okay, Doug. Cleanup crew for two weeks for intimidation. Now get back to your chair and sit up straight. You're in the hot seat again." The counselor leaned back. "And I have plenty of time."

Doug groaned. *What do they want from me? Get off my back. I've already told them everything I know.*

"Tell the group what you did, and why."

"Stole a car. Because I'm a screwup."

Doug looked around the room, then avoided his counselor's eyes. It was the same thing he had said each time before. Doug knew it wasn't enough. He didn't know what else to say.

"Tell us when you started getting in trouble."

"The day I was born," Doug said.

They went back and forth for a while. *Talk about your childhood. Talk about school. Talk about your family. Mom and Dad. How do you feel, Doug? No, how do you really feel? What are you feeling right now?*

"I'm angry," Doug finally screamed. "I wish you'd just lay off."

"That's better," the counselor said. "At least you're being honest with us. Now tell me, Doug—who hurt you. Who hurt you so badly you couldn't say how you felt?"

"Nobody hurt me," Doug said. "Like you said, I've been hurting myself."

"Was it your mom, Doug? Your dad? Both? Who hurt you so much you couldn't feel the pain? What happened? It's okay, Doug. You're safe now. Tell me."

His counselor started telling Doug a story about something that happened when he was a child, something his father had done to him that made him feel so ashamed, so embarrassed, so far away from the rest of the world that he just bypassed the pain. His counselor told him how he ran from that pain, and started acting out because it was his only way of telling himself how much he hurt and how angry he was.

"Who hurt you, Doug? I really want to know. I care about you." His counselor looked into his eyes. It wasn't just words. The counselor meant what he said.

It wasn't a leak. It came out unexpectedly, in a volcanic explosion. Slowly, at first, in bits, then tears, then rage, then more tears, and then the counselor was just holding Doug, holding him and telling him it was going to be okay.

An uncle. His father's brother. So loved and respected by the family. Making Doug touch him, do that to him, every time he got him alone. He kept telling his parents he didn't want to go—didn't want to go hunting with him, didn't want to do jobs for him. His father insisted. Said it would be good for him. Well, it wasn't. And nobody had cared. Nobody had listened to him when he said, *No, I don't want to go.*

Doug cried for hours after telling his secret to his counselor and himself. Then Doug felt strange for days, different from how he could remember feeling for the past ten years.

"Wow," Doug said. "I didn't know all those feelings were there."

Twenty years later, Doug's phone rang. "Doug, we have a new admission from juvenile detention," the admissions secretary said. "Two car thefts; history of school trouble. His name is Jake. I know you can work your magic on him."

Doug saw a seventeen-year-old with dark hair, baggy pants, and a stud in his nose swagger into the room. This kid reminded Doug of himself. Doug saw more than a teenager who was acting out. He saw a person who was angry, hurt, and acting all those emotions out in socially unacceptable ways.

Doug didn't think of himself as having any particular magic. His ability to work with troubled youth had begun to emerge naturally. So had his choice to use the gift of what he had learned to help other teenagers heal from their pain. Doug knew that bad habits take on a life of their own, and that people are responsible for what they do no matter what's been done to them. But he also understood the game of cause and effect as it applies to emotions and therapy.

"Welcome to rehab," Doug said. "I'm your counselor. Go take that stud out of your nose. Then come back in here and we'll talk."

We run from pain in many ways. We deny, pretend, push down, medicate, seek revenge, detach from the part of us that feels, then act out our pain. We cope in the best ways we know. We think we're controlling our lives this way, but we're not. Something that happened *to* us is still controlling us. Sometimes we've pushed the incident so far back we genuinely can't remember it or how we felt.

When I began recovery from chemical dependency, there was an emotional explosion hidden within me that rocked the walls of Wilmar State Hospital when it finally leaked out in 1973. *Wow*, I thought. *I never knew all those feelings were there.*

When I began recovering from codependency, at the first Al-Anon meeting I attended, I was outraged at first. When I found myself sitting in the midst of a group of people who were healthy, loving, and genuinely working on themselves—a place where I felt safe—my denial began to fade. I didn't need it anymore. Soon all I could do was sit there and cry. Underneath all those desperate attempts at compulsive controlling and manipulation was a big wheelbarrow of sorrow and grief. *Wow*, I thought. *I never knew all those feelings were there.*

I still needed help and programs of recovery to get well and to change. I needed recovery programs before, during, and after my emotional explosion. But once all the repressed feelings came exploding or dribbling out, the process of changing my behaviors began to take on a life of its own.

In his book *Brain Lock: Free Yourself from Obsessive-Compulsive Disorder,* Jeffrey M. Schwartz, M.D., told a story about one of his patients who was successfully combating his OCD and the link this patient found between unfelt emotions and compulsive behavior.

"When he is able to do so [feel his feelings] he finds that his OCD level is very low, whereas when he suppresses his feelings his OCD is at its worst.

"For years, he had used medication to bolster therapy, but he came to believe that 'medication was really leveling out my personality. I was just very numb. My feelings were very much kept in check. In order to fight their OCD, people have to really let their feelings go.'"

The patient wasn't able to cry over his mother's death. But he wept when Mickey Mantle died.

There are two kinds of feelings. There are the surface emotions—like the irritation and aggravation that Doug felt when his counselor asked him how he felt. And those can be important clues and links. But for many of us, there are deeper emotions hidden underneath.

Back in the days when I facilitated groups with other counselors in therapeutic communities in Minneapolis, we used to have some real barn burners. We scorched through those top layers until the walls tumbled down. Everyone—the person in the hot seat, the counselors, the other members in the group—left the groups, some of which went on for hours and days, changed.

There was magic in the air.

People didn't talk *about* their feelings.

They felt how they felt.

The ability to detach from our emotions is a human survival safety device. It protects us from feelings that are too overwhelming to feel until we can sort out how to protect ourselves in other ways.

Part of staying present for each step means choosing to stay present for how we really feel. Ouch. That hurts. Yeah, and it probably has for a long time. If we skipped a step or two when we were children, staying present now means going back and feeling how we felt back then.

---

*Healing old emotional wounds is a grueling
but miracle-working choice.*

6

She Missed a Step, Too

———

It happened in a flurry, as accidents sometimes do. One minute she was stepping out of the shower. In the next moment, the phone and doorbell rang—both at the same time. Carol grabbed her robe and headed for the stairs leading to the main level of her apartment. That dang yipping dog jumped under her foot. She wasn't paying attention. Going too fast. Whoops. She missed a step. Lost her balance. Tumbled all the way down.

For a moment she was stunned. It had all happened so quickly. She tried to stand up. She couldn't. She looked at her leg.

She knew it was broken.

God, it really hurt.

Two days later, the hospital released her and sent her home with a huge bottle of pain medication and orders to rest. She lay on the couch in her living room, glaring at the foot of the stairs.

I've really hit bottom in my life, she thought. She looked at the bottle of pain pills. Take one or two every six hours as needed. She swallowed two and considered a third. *Why do bad things all happen at once?* she wondered, waiting for the medication to kick in. She had waited seven years for Michael to come around. He had come around—for a while. Then he'd go back to his ex-wife. Then he'd come back to her.

It was an unfulfilling revolving door.

So was the treatment center where he frequently went to deal with his recurring addiction to coke.

How stupid have I been to wait around pathetically all those years? What was I thinking of? We had some good times, but all the guy brought me was misery and pain. She looked at her leg. *Kind of like that.*

She had finally broken it off three months ago. *Now he's gone. For good. And I'm stuck here, still in pain, still waiting, still alone.*

Two weeks passed, then three. Money was tight. Her leg still hurt. The break had been severe. The doctor had supplied her with all the pain medication she needed. It was so tempting to just lie on the couch and sink into euphoria. The pills helped the throbbing in her leg. And they numbed the pain in her heart.

She reached for another pill. A quiet voice said, *Watch out. You're getting addicted, too.*

For two more days, Carol lay there gobbling pain pills like they were M&M's. It was a Wednesday, when she got up to hobble on crutches to the refrigerator to get a soda, that she realized she couldn't remember the last time her mind had been clear. She had been in a medicated stupor ever since the accident.

If I keep going this way, I'll end up in treatment, too, she thought, heading for the phone. *There must be another way. My leg really hurts, but I can't keep gobbling these pills.*

She called her doctor.

The following Monday she took a taxi to an address her doctor gave her. It was a clinic that helped people non-chemically manage physical pain. She went to the groups and therapy sessions. She began to learn how to live with the pain and relax herself without medication, so it didn't hurt as much. She was still in a cast. Her leg still hurt. She had still wasted the last seven years of her life.

And all it had led to was learning to manage the pain.

The clinic she attended was seven days long, an outpatient one. Follow-up was available for several months. Carol went back once or twice a week, as needed, for continued help.

It was there she met Jason. He had attended a pain clinic, too. He was a mountain climber, and on his last climb he had injured his back.

"Let's go out for dinner and talk about how good life can be when you're not in pain," he said.

Carol agreed.

Sixteen months later, Carol stepped out of the shower, dried herself off, put on her robe, got dressed, and then carefully went down the stairs. She didn't want to slip today. She was marrying Jason in four hours.

"How'd you two meet?" an aunt asked at the reception following the wedding.

Carol was silent for a moment, wondering what to say. Choosing to end an unfulfilling relationship, finally after all those years. Not paying attention. Falling down the steps. That dang yipping dog. Breaking her leg. Taking too much medication for too much pain. Deciding to stop taking it. Needing help. Choosing to follow through with that plan.

"A lot of very strange twists of fate," she finally said. "I'll tell you all about it someday."

Sometimes we can miss a step and things still work out if we stay present for all the steps that come after that.

Some people spend years looking for the magic everywhere they go. Often they end up frustrated and disappointed because they miss the beauty of what's there. Stop looking so hard. Mind your own business. Pay attention to each decision and detail in your life. Be present for each moment. Let the magic come to you.

Remember the words of Dr. Seuss in *Oh, the Places You Will Go?*

"Today is your day! Your mountain is waiting. So. . . Get on your way."

———

Anything can happen. Anything at all.

7

She Laughed Away the Gray

Ginny looked in the mirror. *Another gray hair. Actually, another ten of them*, she thought, plucking them out one by one.

She stared in the mirror, then scowled. Where had the twenty-year-old woman gone? She still felt her, inside this fifty-year-old body.

She pulled at the skin underneath her eyes. Hmm. Should I get a face-lift, get my lips pulled back to my ears? Or should I do this thing naturally?

I just don't know, she thought. *Guess I'll wait and see.*

The phone rang. It was her daughter.

"Mom, please come over and hang out with me. Please. Please. Please," her daughter begged. Lately that's all she seemed to want.

"No, honey. You need to have your own life now. I need to have mine."

They talked for a long time. Finally Ginny hung up the phone and laughed. It wasn't always this way. When her daughter moved out, their relationship had been impossibly tense. They barely talked, and when they did, it was strained. It had taken her a while to catch on to what was taking place.

She was going through the syndrome called *empty nest.*

"I felt hurt, rejected, angry, and confused," Ginny said. "I couldn't figure out what was going on. For all of her life, I had been the most important person in the world to this little girl. She was my life, too. Suddenly she barely had time to talk to me. I wasn't important to her, not at all, anymore.

"I was secretly jealous of all her new friends. They were getting all the love she once gave to me.

"I had tried to be the best mom I could. All she did was push me away and point out all the things I had done wrong. One day I realized what was going on. She was establishing her identity separate from me. This pushing away of me was what she needed to do. The harder I tried to cling to her, the more she pushed. It was really tough. It hurt a lot. But I had to let her go."

Ginny stopped waiting for her baby to come home. Instead, she took some of that love and learned to baby herself. She took trips, went places, and did things she could never before even imagine.

"Guess what?" Ginny said. "My baby came back. But when she did, she was a grown woman and I had a new life. I miss our times as a family, when she lived at home and was a little girl. They were difficult times a lot of the time. Maybe the best times of my life. But this time is good, too. We love each other as much or more than we ever did now. It's not better or worse, just different.

"It's the next part of both of our lives."

So now you're getting older.

What are you going to do? Tummy tuck? Eye lift? Maybe a bottle of hair dye? Or go the natural way and laugh away the gray?

Guess what?

That's your choice, too.

8

He Was Sick of Being Sick

"A colostomy? You mean wear a bag that I go to the bathroom in? No," Ralph said. "Absolutely not. No way. What are my other options?"

The doctor explained that Ralph could go through chemotherapy and radiation and not have the colostomy. He could choose not to have any of the surgeries. Or he could go through chemo and radiation and have the colostomy, which was what he, the doctor, recommended as the best route.

"I've got to go home and think about this," Ralph said. "I'll get back to you later."

Ralph drove home, not saying much to his wife sitting next to him.

Where had his life gone? He had been in perfect health until one day last spring. It started with stomach pain. Then the doctors had discovered cancer in his stomach. They had taken that out, said he was fine. Then when he went back in for a checkup, they discovered more cancer, this time in his colon. It was all getting to be too much. Way too much. He hadn't felt good for over eight months.

Now this doctor was telling him he wanted him to wear a bag?

"Honey, I want you around," his wife said. "But it's your body and your life. You decide what you want to do."

It's hard to get sick. It can affect our emotions, our relationships, our faith, and our quality of life. It's another time when it helps to hunker down, pull out our emergency self-care procedures, and gently take care of ourselves the best that we can.

We don't have to be getting older for our bodies to break down. Some people are born with physical handicaps. Some people get very sick, very young. Some people live to be one hundred with almost no physical ailments at all.

I've known people who were paralyzed and people with no legs who jump out of airplanes. I know one man who had a colostomy years ago. He's in his early seventies now. He drives to the drop zone each day—on a motorcycle—and jumps out of a plane just to keep himself young.

I know another woman who had a serious form of polio and spent most of her young and adult life in a nursing home, so severely handicapped that she'd be stuck on the toilet for hours until a nursing assistant remembered her and came to help. When she turned fifty, she rented her own apartment. She has a boyfriend now. Because of her physical handicaps and his, they hire a sex aid in order to make love.

I know a woman who's lived with HIV for years. She's young, beautiful, and has a safe and active love life (both romantic and with friends). She has more suitors than most women I know.

Broken down or in great shape, it's your body.

People can tell us what to eat and when—no cholesterol, low cholesterol, the Zone, no meat, lots of pasta, no eggs. Sometimes it seems like everyone says a different thing. At any given time in history, something on the food shelves at the grocery store screams, *Don't eat me or you'll die.*

We can listen to what the doctor says. We can get a second, third, and fourth opinion. We can go holistic or Western medicine or a combination of both. We can take whatever medicine a doctor gives us or we can ask questions and get information.

———————

But if we're over eighteen, deciding what to do with,
what to put into, and how to medically treat our bodies
is our choice and ours alone.

9

She Rode the Wheel

————

When you learn your lessons, the pain goes away. That's what she wrote in *The Wheel of Life*.

The famous *Death and Dying* lady lay on the hospital bed in her living room. She couldn't get up. A series of strokes—nineteen or more—had left her severely handicapped. Paralyzed on one side. It was morning. She was thirsty. Elisabeth Kübler-Ross said a quick prayer. "God, please send someone. A cup of tea would be so nice."

I got lost on the back roads in Arizona. Even with a navigation system in my car, I couldn't find the address. I bumped around on the roads in my four-wheel drive. The woman with me, Lori, frowned.

"Haven't you ever been four-wheeling before?" I asked.

"No," she said.

"Then it's time." She had quit her job as a reporter at the *Miami Herald*. Now she was freelancing and writing a book. Together we were on our way to interview Elisabeth Kübler-Ross. I don't have a lot of female heroes in this world. Elisabeth is definitely one. She had done so much groundbreaking work on the subject of grief, death, dying, and life after death. And I wanted to meet her before she died.

Finally we found the address. Rang the doorbell. "Come in," Elisabeth yelled. We pushed open the door.

"Hi, Elisabeth," I said. "Would you like me to make you a cup of tea?"

We helped fix her some food. She asked me to help her put her shorts on. Carefully I did as she asked.

"It's about receiving," she said. "I never learned to receive. Now God has put me in a position where I have no choice but to ask for and accept help."

I helped her get in the wheelchair, pushed her into the bathroom. I looked away, trying to give her some privacy while she washed her face and brushed her teeth.

I pushed her back to the living room. Lori and I sat down in front of her.

"Go ahead," she said. "Ask away."

Lori cleared her throat. "I've been researching a book. I'm trying to find out what it means to own my power."

"That's easy, my dear," Elisabeth said. "All you have to do is be who you are."

Elisabeth looked at me. "And you," she said. "What do you want to ask?"

Now it was my turn to clear my throat.

"Do you really believe in life after death? Aren't you afraid of death, at least a little bit?" I asked.

Elisabeth laughed. "Didn't you read my book, dear?" she said. "It's not about believing. I know there's life after death. Dying is the easy part. It's life that's hard."

We said our good-byes. Elisabeth did what she called an ET touch—gently extending her finger, as any more touch than that caused her pain.

I leaned over and whispered in her ear, "Thank you. And have a safe trip home."

Lessons. Lessons. And more lessons. Every step of the way there's something to learn. Just when you think you've got them all under your belt, another lesson comes blowing your way.

Some of them come disguised as problems or issues to solve. Others are normal effects caused by life and by getting older each day. Within each category of lessons, there are many little mini-lessons, too.

Fear can be a fun lesson to learn. I started jumping out of airplanes as part of learning about that. Play is an enjoyable lesson too—although some of us are stiff and forced at first. Some people's lesson is to stop playing and learn to work. Some of the other lessons aren't as pleasurable. They hurt when they're happening to us. Grief, a broken heart, hurts physically and emotionally, and can go on for a long, long time. The pain from loss and grief can take two to eight years—sometimes more.

Guilt is the worst. Absolutely the worst. The feeling is paralyzing, and we often push it down so deep inside of us we're not even aware it's there. But the thoughts keep floating through our mind.

It's like being in a relationship with the most tormentive person on the planet. Constantly our guilt is telling us: you don't deserve, people might find out, you can't be who you are. Sometimes it can take us to the edge: you don't deserve to be happy; you don't deserve to live. It's subtle and insidious. Even if we tell it to shut up, it still stares at us with condemning eyes.

Some of us not only have guilt as a lesson, we have guilt about the lessons we find ourselves going through. Guilt permeates our lives.

I thought the concept of lessons was interesting as a general idea—until these lessons kept happening to *me*. I kept waiting for the lessons to stop. And I would have moments of rest, play, respite. Until the winds blew another lesson my way.

Well, this is fine, I'd think. *Let's just get it over so I can get my piece of the pie, get my share of the dream.* In the *Big Book of Alcoholics Anonymous,* Bill Wilson talks about happy, joyous, and free. I wanted to get to that part. And each time I'd get another lesson under my belt, I'd think, *now I'm finally there.* Until the next lesson began.

At a seminar in Pasadena in 2001, the Dalai Lama said that all people want the same thing—they just want to be happy.

That's what the big grinding Wheel of Life is trying to do—get us to that place of being happy and free. We do get the big brass ring—but it's often not what we thought it would be. Sometimes slowly, sometimes in a flash of transformation, we get it—whatever the lesson we're going through is. After years of waiting, we finally become so patient we forget that we're waiting and what we're waiting for. After years of trying to control everything around us, we wear ourselves out and finally surrender. After years of keeping our hearts hardened and afraid, we become flooded with forgiveness, tolerance, and compassion. After years of grasping at other people, we finally feel content and complete taking care of ourselves.

After years of being selfish and not considering anyone but ourselves, we learn to give. Or the opposite may be true. After years of giving everything away, we allow ourselves to become vulnerable and receive, too.

Experience. It's both a noun and a verb. Things happen to us, and we immerse ourselves in those scenarios. We dive in. Go through it. Submerge. Then come out changed—or not. We may go around and around the lesson wheel again and again, sometimes at different levels, until we *get* the lesson being taught.

––––––––

The lesson may be over, but don't forget what you learned.
You're going to need it while you climb mountain number two.

BRINGING HEAVEN TO EARTH

"Choices? Hard calls?" a friend, Dan Cain, said one day. "They're really not that difficult. Initially I made my choices based on what was best only for me. By that I mean my choices were self-serving, compulsive. *Me, me, me.* Later, with some luck, and having lived a long enough life, I reached the realization that life is paradoxical. The less emphasis on me, the more there actually was for me.

"All the clichés are true," he said. "Tell the truth, you won't have so much to remember. There's no free lunch. You get what you pay for. If you set out in search of God, be sure to pack a lunch. If you simply practice the Golden Rule, God will come to you."

They help hold the world and the heaven together, wrote the poet Li Bai when he saw the nine brilliant mountains and ninety-nine peaks of Jiuhua Shan—holy mountain number two.

"I can already tell that this is going to be my favorite mountain," Joe said when the bus pulled into the village that sat tucked at the mountain's base.

I didn't know it yet, but Jiuhua Shan was going to be my favorite, too.

It was raining when we began climbing the steps. The higher the altitude, the tougher the climb. At 1,342 meters, this climb would be more intense than the last. Focusing on each step helped. The stairs led up, then they'd wind back down. *Ugh*, I'd think. *Whenever we go down, it means we have to go back up again.*

We climbed for hours, and then stopped at a stand to rest. The incline was steep now. It was like climbing a ladder into the heavens—straight up, with very steep and narrow steps. Each step required more energy and more focus than the last.

He appeared from nowhere—a thin man, carrying wooden beams on his back. He couldn't have weighed more than 155 pounds. He didn't look that strong, but he was determined to carry what looked like almost his weight—or more—in wooden beams up those steps.

"For temple at top," he said, nodding and smiling.

We got into a pattern with him, stopping at the same snack stands, and then getting back on the stairs again. At one stand, Joe and I bought him a banana and a soda.

"It's the least we can do," Joe said. "I can't believe you're carrying all that weight up these steps."

I marveled at the man's strength and determination as we neared the top of the peak. I was exhausted, strained beyond what I felt I could endure by the altitude and the sheer severity of the climb. Each step taxed every muscle and fiber in my body. Yet somehow I was given the strength to keep climbing.

So was he.

I looked at the pile of bills I had tucked away in the drawer. The marriage had left me fifty thousand dollars in debt. I earned eight hundred dollars a month, and I had two children to support. How would I ever do it? By making a decision to take responsibility for yourself, *that quiet voice said*. By doing the best you can. By taking it one step at a time. Slowly I chipped away at the bills. I talked honestly with my creditors. At some point, a force set in. A momentum was gained. I reached the top of that mountain. I became debt-free.

This force worked the other way, too. When I was addicted to alcohol and drugs, I wondered how I would get my next fix. From the middle of nowhere in St. Paul, Minnesota, in 1969 I was able to find heroin, cocaine—every drug I needed to keep getting high.

Whenever I made a choice for good or for ill, that choice itself had been the starting point. A force then kicked in that moved me along, bringing to pass the events I needed to turn a simple thought into reality. Like climbing the mountain, the journey might have strained and taxed me, evoked powerful emotions along the way. But in retrospect, what had looked impossible repeatedly became a possibility by the choices I made.

I watched the man reach the top of the mountain carrying the wooden beams on his back. *Ordinary people are capable of extraordinary deeds—good or evil—by making a choice and then taking one step at a time.*

We reached the top of the mountain, looked around, and then rested for a while. When we made it back down to the village, it was dark. We stopped at a small grocery store to buy something to eat for supper before returning to the guest house at the monastery. I selected three items—a package of cookies, a container of dehydrated noodle bowl, and a banana. The man behind the counter totaled my purchases. He wrote the amount I owed him on a slip. I looked at it, and then figured out the dollar amount he was asking for in American currency. Twenty dollars for soup, cookies, and a banana? I argued with him about the price. He insisted twenty dollars was right. I was in a bind now. This was the only grocery store open in town and I was starved. I pushed the items back toward him on the counter, shook my head no, turned, and began walking out the door. He started hollering at me, and then wrote some new numbers down on a piece of paper. Now my purchases totaled $2.50. *That's more like it,* I thought.

Early the next morning, we boarded the bus to return to Wuhu. The bus was about half-filled with passengers. A group of us watched with amusement as one woman diligently managed to keep other passengers from sitting next to her. She had placed her purse in the seat next to her. Each time we stopped to let more passengers board, they would walk to where she sat, look at the empty seat next to her, notice it filled with her purse, then walk away and select another seat. She didn't look up. If they stood there too long, looking at the seat occupied by her purse, she would just point at her purse as if to say, *You can't sit in that seat. It's occupied.*

Finally all the seats on the bus were filled except for the seat next to this woman, the one occupied by her purse. The bus stopped. A girl about thirteen boarded. She was pretty, dressed in the latest fashionable sneakers and jeans. She had a sweet, innocent look about her. She walked to the one available seat, next to this woman, and then noticed the woman's purse in it. The woman shook her head no, pointing to her purse. The girl stood there waiting, looking confused.

The bus driver had obviously been watching this woman, too. He put the bus in park, stood up, walked back to the seat occupied by the purse, snatched up the purse, put it in the woman's lap, then motioned for the girl to sit in the seat where the purse had been.

The passengers began applauding. The woman looked embarrassed and uncomfortable. At the next stop, she scurried off the bus.

As the bus took me farther and farther away from the village, I noticed a sadness settling in. By the time we arrived back at Wuhu, I was downright agitated and depressed. It surprised me, because whatever feeling I had experienced at Jiuhua had been so subtle that I hadn't noticed it until it was gone.

That's what it is, I thought. *Visiting Jiuhua had been like visiting heaven. Now that I was gone, I missed the feeling I had found so naturally there. What the guidebook had said had been true: a palpable spirituality permeated the air. This depression, this heaviness, this agitation is the emptiness we feel when we're away from God.*

Manipulation. Lies. Con artists. Everyone wants something for themselves. People betray each other. And sometimes we betray them and ourselves.

People can be so loving, so kind. They can also be downright mean.

There's a lot of gravity on planet earth.

It's easy to look around and think, *I've got to be careful. Just do for me and mine.* Or we notice the emptiness inside ourselves, see an ad for that new car, and think, "Oh, that's what will make me happy and fill this empty spot."

What most of us really want is not just more things or another relationship. As Rabbi Philip S. Berg says, we want our relationships, work, and possessions to be part of our happiness.

We want our choices to work.

Every religion in the world and every spiritual program that I've studied, been involved in, or practiced has espoused one consistent truth: the place where we're farthest away from heaven is when we're only serving ourselves—when we're wanting more and more of everything and just wanting it for ourselves. Whether we call it self-serving, plain selfishness, or self-will, it's the same unhappy place.

Don't take my word for it. Try an experiment. See for yourself. Go to the grocery store. Buy all the trimmings for a Thanksgiving dinner. Then cook a turkey, potatoes, gravy, stuffing, and a pie. Don't forget the cranberries. Now sit down at your table and eat that dinner alone—all by yourself.

Not much fun, is it?

Now invite some family or friends over—maybe a couple of strangers, too. People who are hungry, lonely, tired, or poor. Invite them to partake in your feast. Talk with them. Laugh. Be genuinely interested in them.

See what I mean?

It's the old-fashioned way. It's been around for years. If you're thinking of yourself and wondering why you don't have enough, better, or more—the secret is to be of service to somebody else.

In this section we'll look at stories about people who made choices that served others and reflected reasonable concern for themselves. Intentions are a powerful force. We can react to all this misery and hatefulness by becoming selfish, mean and self-serving, or we can take action and become a cause for love.

Making that hard call is how we create heaven on earth.

1

She Made a Hard Call

———

Brenda walked down the hallway to the administrative offices, staring at all the pictures on the wall. The governor congratulating the president of the organization. Three staff members onstage with some celebrities, shaking hands. Plaques and media clips raving about what a wonderful service organization this was.

What a crock, Brenda thought, sitting down at her desk. *If they only knew.*

"Everybody skims off the top," her boss had said. "It's no big deal. It's a perk we get for being in the service industry. They don't pay us enough to live. It's how we get rewarded for all our hard work."

Brenda had been writing the checks for *perks* for months now. It was her job. *It would be so much easier if I was just a stranger, someone cold they'd brought in*, she thought. *The problem is, these people who are stealing are my friends.*

She tried to look the other way. Today she stared the problem right in the face. A client had pulled her aside, complained about the lack of services he was getting and the quality of the food the program was serving to him.

"I'm sick of this slop, Brenda," he said. "And I'm hungry all the time. What's the deal? Why can't they feed us right here?"

Brenda had hemmed and hawed. Inside she was boiling. The reason the clients weren't getting fed is because the people at the top were getting fat. Money that was supposed to be going one place was going someplace else. She stared at the phone. If she picked it up and made that call—reported the agency to the powers that be—the program would close. She'd be out of a job—and this was work she had wanted to do for a long time. Her friends would be out of work, too. They might never work in this field again. If she didn't make the call the agency would continue to do its work in the world, and some of that work was valuable and good.

She wished she could just stay numb, keep looking the other way. But the anger boiling inside her today was too much to deny. The clients were dependent on this program to meet their needs while they were here; they were vulnerable adults.

She hauled out the phone book, looked up the number. Her hands were sweating as she picked up the phone.

"I'd like to talk to someone in the licensing department," she said. "I work for a social-services program and I have an internal problem to report—one you might want to investigate."

When she hung up the phone she still felt anxious, guilty, and scared. A lot of unknowns had just come into play—her job, her future, her relationships with her friends. But oddly enough, another feeling ran deeper than those. *Peace.* For the first time in months she got a good night's sleep.

She was going to have to live with a lot of problems in her future, but at least she could live with herself.

• • •

What is our responsibility? What isn't? What are our intentions? What's right? What's wrong? How involved should we become? Which path do we take? Neither option feels good. But one feels *really* wrong.

————

That's why they're called hard calls.

2

He Found Peace in a War Zone

———

Marvin sat at the dining room table, looking at the war zone.

His daughter was screaming at his fiancée. "You're not my mother. You can't tell me what to do."

Her daughter was glaring at him.

He and his fiancée were glaring at each other.

This was his cue. He had tried to make this relationship work, but they had hit a wall. Her kid. My kid. Enemy camp. He couldn't take it anymore. And he didn't need this crap in his life.

It was so simple when I was alone, raising my daughter, being a single dad, Marvin thought, getting up from the table. *This is all so complicated. Family histories, family business that doesn't have anything to do with me. I just want peace and quiet again. I want my life back.*

He watched his fiancée gather up the dishes from the table.

The problem is, he thought, *I really love her.*

He grabbed his jacket and went outside for a long walk.

It wasn't any deep soul-searching moment, just a quiet prayer. *It looks like I've only got two choices, God,* he said. *Live in a war zone, or lose the woman I love.*

Neither alternative felt acceptable to him.

He walked back to the house. He helped his fiancée finish cleaning the kitchen, kissed her cheek, and said he was going to bed. She said goodnight; she was going home. An unsettled tension filled the air. He knew this wasn't hard just on him; it was hard on the woman he loved, too. It was a quiet moment of surrender when he chose to say to himself, *I don't know what to do.*

That night he lay in bed, searching through his past. He'd been through a lot in his life. Getting sober, turning his life around. Going through a divorce. Now he was the head of a large company. Listening to people, helping them solve their problems, was a way of life for him. But he couldn't seem to find the solution for the problems he was having with the people he loved most in his life.

Marvin searched his mind for a pattern of problem solving that had worked for him in the past. What were the common denominators every time he hit a wall, and finally broke through? He could find only two. Well, actually three. Make a commitment. Let go. Then find a way to serve and help people by what he was committing to do.

An idea occurred to him, a choice he hadn't thought of before.

It was going to take time, commitment, and energy, but it just might work.

The next day, he called his fiancée at work.

She liked the idea, too.

Within three months, they were leading an informal support group for other families trying to blend. Every other group was open, so the children could attend, too. The group met for over two years. It gave those families the time and space to air their feelings and support each other through change.

Marvin has been married to the woman who was his fiancée for twelve years. "I didn't have a clue if my idea would work or not," Marvin says. "But holding the door open for others—helping other people—was how I learned the skills to be able to walk through that door myself."

Holding the door open for others is a concept that's been around for a long time. It's the foundation of organizations such as Alcoholics Anonymous and other self-help groups.

Life is better when it's shared, and that includes problems. Sometimes we hear an idea we haven't thought of before, or gain a new perspective on what we're going through. Other times, just hearing that other people feel the way we feel validates us, helps us accept ourselves, calms us enough to keep going.

We find courage, strength, and inspiration that we can't find by ourselves.

I stopped by the coffee shop one day and ran into a friend who's involved with a Twelve-Step program. He was sitting with a man who wasn't involved with Twelve-Step groups and didn't have much understanding of them. My friend was trying to explain to this man why he kept working with newcomers to his particular Twelve-Step group.

"I'm not doing it to save their lives," he explained. "I'm doing it to save mine. When I help them, I hear myself telling them what I need to do myself."

There's magic in service. There's magic in a group.

If we want to get it for ourselves, we need to give it away.

Hard calls don't always mean just two choices. Sometimes there's a third: we can ask God to show us what to do.

3

And Goodwill Toward Men

Marlyss put the last wrapped package under the Christmas tree and then stood back to admire her work. The tree was five feet tall, brimming with presents underneath. She hoped it would be a good holiday this year. God had been very good to her. She had one beautiful daughter. She patted her tummy. And another one on the way. She lived in a beautiful house. Her family was in good health. And her husband had a good job, good enough that she didn't have to work. She could stay home and be a full-time mother.

For the most part, she felt blessed.

She didn't know why he had to tell her. She could have lived much better without knowing the details. But he had this great need to come to her one day and confess that he'd had an affair during one of the rough spots in their marriage. They had been to therapy, but things hadn't been the same.

For a lot of reasons, she decided to stay. She didn't want to rip her family apart. And she loved her husband, a lot. She thought of him not just as her lover, but also as her best friend. Sometimes they got along famously since the incident occurred. Sometimes spats and fights arose out of nowhere. They'd fight about the stupidest things. But she knew what they were really arguing about—the affair she'd found out he had.

She had made her choice to stay. She wasn't a victim; she knew that. And she really tried to let go of what happened. But it was hard and took a lot of work. Sometimes she'd look at him and be flooded with love. Other times she'd look at him and it would be like staring at a stranger. *Who is this man?* she'd think. *Do I even know this person I sleep next to every night?*

She worried it would happen again.

Sometimes her fear made her mean.

She looked at the stack of presents under the tree, vacillating between feeling sorry for herself and blessed. Then an image of the old man who lived three houses away flashed through her mind. *Do I really have the energy to care about anyone except my child and myself?* She argued with herself for a while and then walked into the kitchen, put on her apron, and baked for the next two hours.

When she finished the cookies, she put them in a Tupperware container and put a cheery red bow on the top. She called a teenager in the neighborhood and asked her if she could baby-sit for a while.

Then she took the cookies over to the neighbor's house and knocked on his door. Over the intercom, she identified herself. She knew he wouldn't answer the door; he was confined to bed.

"Want some company?" she asked.

"Always," he barked.

She handed him the cookies—peanut butter, his favorite—then pulled a chair up next to his bed. They talked about his kids. He had three grown daughters. "I don't get to see them very often, but that's okay," he said. "They're busy with their own lives. I know how that goes. But they're bringing me over to their home for Christmas Day."

He talked about his grandchildren, what they liked, how good they made him feel when they called him Pops.

Then he started reminiscing about his wife.

She had died seven years ago. He had lived alone since then. He didn't believe in any of what he called this nonsense about life after death. He felt sad and alone, because he believed in his heart he'd never see his wife again.

It bothered Marlyss when he talked this way. She believed strongly in life after death. He and she had discussed it before. But she bit her tongue and just listened to him talk. She had come over here to comfort him, not to convert him to her way of thought.

Hot tea, cookies, and conversation made two hours pass quickly. She noticed he was getting tired, and she realized it was time for her to go. "Merry Christmas," she said.

She went home. All the problems she had before were still there. She didn't know how those problems would be resolved. She didn't know if she'd get slammed with a betrayal again. But her step felt a little lighter. She had a smile on her face. It wasn't so hard to stay away from the obsessive thinking that drove her nuts.

She walked to the stereo and put on a CD.

"Joy to the World" filled her house.

I am not naive enough to believe that baking cookies for a neighbor will solve or sort out marital problems—or any other problem, for that matter. And there are times when many of us need to back off from giving for a while, because compulsive giving nearly ruined our lives.

We don't always know how a situation will work out. Sometimes it takes a while—a long time—for relationship problems to resolve themselves. No matter how hard we try, it can be hard to *hang on loose* when there's a potential problem looming. But one of the best cures for thinking too much about if and when we're going

to be hurt again is to forget about ourselves for a moment and do
something nice for someone else.

————————

While you're at it, don't give something that makes you happy,
give something you believe will make them *happy to receive.*

4

He Got What He Paid For

They had only had a two-week fling. He hadn't talked to her or seen her since. He didn't even know why he called her that day. It was just a feeling he had.

"How are you?" he asked.

"Pretty good," she said. "I just got home from the hospital."

"The hospital? What's wrong?"

"I just had a baby," she said.

Jerry could feel goose bumps rising on his skin as he started counting backward in his head. She didn't have to say what she did next. He already knew. That baby was his.

He hung up the phone, paced for a few minutes. Then he got in his car and drove as fast as he could. The moment he saw the baby, Jerry knew it was his son.

He gently picked him up and kissed him from the top of his head to the bottom of his feet.

"I wanted to make him mine," he said.

It was hard learning to be a dad. At first Jerry would just visit, hang out, be around him for a while. But as soon as his son got older—about a year and a half—Jerry began spending as much time with him as he could—three or four days a week. "I'm sorry my son has a broken family," he said. "But what I can do is give him more than my money. I can give him my time, energy, and love."

For a twenty-one-year-old, he was wise. He knew one of the most important secrets of life: you get what you pay for every time. Whether it's at work, a hobby, or a relationship, you're going to get back from something only what you put into it.

I was talking to a woman one day. She was young, in her early twenties. She had just had her first baby and had gone through a difficult time—up all day and night for months on end. She kept trying to find time for her career that first year she was raising her child, wondering if there were any books out for new moms about how to make more time for themselves.

"I realized something," she said. "All this energy, all this getting up in the middle of the night, all this struggling to learn what to do has bonded me to this child in a way I couldn't imagine."

Starting something new? A job? A recovery program? Or maybe you're not getting the satisfaction you'd like out of your family or career. Yes, you may be with the wrong person. Or you may not like your job and the solution may be to work somewhere else. But if you're there today, why not try a novel approach?

———

Put a little more of yourself into whatever you do.

5

She Got a Tip

———

Leslie looked at the clock. Thank God. Her shift at the restaurant was almost done. She brought the bills to the last two tables, joked with her customers for a few seconds, then went into the back room.

Time to go home. Not really home. She worked a second job, too. But at least this job was done.

It had been hard juggling her schedule since her daughter had become so ill. She had been in the hospital now for over a month. The doctors didn't know if she was going to make it. So far, the bone-marrow transplant seemed to be taking. But Leslie knew one thing: you never know for sure.

Leslie's boyfriend, Eddy, was sweet. He was there for her, and he was there for her children, too. But he didn't make that much money. And these weren't his children. She looked in the mirror. A little overweight. Oh well. Right now, food was about the only relief she had.

She walked across the restaurant and headed for the door. Her boss motioned for her to come talk to him. She lumbered over. God, she was tired. Sometimes she didn't know how tired she was until she was about to get off her feet. He was a good boss. He gave her a lot of flexibility. He treated his employees well.

She smiled at him.

"Someone left this for you," he said. "I don't know what it is."

He handed her an envelope. It was the size of a greeting card. She wondered for a moment. *It's Valentine's Day. One of my customers probably left me a card,* she thought. She stuck it in her purse, headed home, and sank into a tub full of hot water. She had two hours to rest.

Leslie made herself a pot of coffee and then remembered the card. She opened it up. Fifteen one-hundred-dollar bills fell out.

The message on the card was simple: "We know you're going through a hard time right now. Don't stop being such a sweet person. And please don't stop believing in God. Happy Valentine's Day from people you've served."

I was at a speaking engagement in Washington, D.C. A woman raised her hand.

"Ms. Beattie! Ms. Beattie!" she said. "I'm new to this whole game of figuring out what it means to take care of myself. I don't really get it. Do you mean that we need to just take care of ourselves for a while, until we meet somebody that will take care of us?"

Most of the people in the room giggled.

"Ummm, no," I said. "But I know how you feel. The thing about taking care of ourselves is that it's pretty much a lifetime job."

I can remember lying in bed next to my now ex-husband, staring at the wall, knowing something was very wrong but not knowing what it was. Did you ever hear stories about people who swore they spotted the Virgin Mary? They'd see a splotch on a subway wall or on the floor, and this splotch took on the shape of a holy figure? Well, the longer I stared at this wall, the longer the splotch looked like a picture of Jesus. It was a stupid thing, I know. But the point is, I'd stare at it and wonder why God felt so far away, why God had just left me on my own like this.

It took a lot more months and years of grinding through the lessons I was going through to understand that God hadn't abandoned me.

I had abandoned myself.

Sometimes I think we see what we need to see to help ourselves climb the next step.

I had given so much to so many people. I felt so guilty about everything I had done wrong. I just didn't know how to say no without adding to the pile of guilt I already felt. And I truly didn't want to hurt anyone, or make anyone any more upset with me than I already was with myself.

I didn't get this thing called giving. I knew that I was finally in a program of recovery for my chemical dependency. I had been selfish, confused, and self-centered all my life. And it was important for me to finally think of somebody other than myself.

All this giving, this compulsive giving, backfired. Well, it didn't really backfire. It helped save me from chemical dependency. But it also sent me to Al-Anon. There's a way to give and be of service that's healthy. And there's a way to give that doesn't work as well.

I had to back off from giving for a while. I had to learn the difference between giving as a *reaction* and giving as an *action*. I had to learn to take care of and give to myself, too.

As a child, I wasn't allowed to say no. It was important for me to learn to say that word as an adult. It was important for me to learn what it meant to stand up for myself, call people on their *stuff*, recognize when I was being lied to and manipulated, and realize that although God would do for me what I couldn't do for myself, I was expected to do what I could.

When my book *Codependent No More* became successful, a lot of people expected a lot from me. I expected a lot from myself. I didn't know that much. I was a simple journalist, self-taught. And I had just shared a few ideas that had helped me.

Because I had been so poor financially, the success of that book brought me a lifestyle change—including a lot of *things*. I was able to pay my bills, buy a new car if I wanted, and buy new clothes. I was able to give a lot more to people, too.

The downside of that was that a lot of people saw that I had money. I'm sure they thought, *Why her and not me?* I thought that, too. You see, we don't say, *Why did that happen to me?* only when bad things happen. Many of us say that when something good happens, too.

I don't know why I was blessed financially. I don't know why by the Grace of God I was allowed to recover from chemical dependency when so many people don't. I don't know why my son had to die.

I don't know why I'm still alive.

But this much I have learned along the path: it's really easy to convince ourselves that things, and a relationship, and a beautiful home will make us happy. And don't get me wrong, those things are nice. But it wasn't the things that ever made me happy. The only *thing* that has ever brought my heart any sense of permanent joy are those moments when I have felt blessed by God and the moments when I opened my heart and risked love.

After my son died, it was hard for me to care about life. It was hard for me to care about whether the work I did helped other people or not. Maybe backing off from the world was exactly what I needed to do for a while. There was a night onstage in New Jersey. I was supposed to follow Deepak Chopra and speak. The speaking engagement got a little confused. The room was hot. By the time I got up on the stage it was late. I looked at the sea of faces in the audience. The only thing, the only thing in my heart, I had to say was "There are moments when life really sucks."

I couldn't fake my way through this one. I might have had experience to share. But I didn't have much hope. I just looked at all the people out there and said, "It's late. I don't have much to say. I'm going back to my hotel and going to bed."

I didn't think I'd ever be happy again. I'll most likely never be happy that my son died, nor will I understand *why*. But the point of all this story, and the point of what I went through, is that no matter how bad life was for me, when I was ready to come back to life, the only way I could do that was to give up my self-serving attitudes and practice the only way I know to get a life, and that's to give and to serve.

Maybe some of you need to back off from giving for a while. Maybe you wish that someone would come along and just take care of you. I feel that way sometimes. But every time I relinquish the job, I end up taking it back. There is a way to respect and honor ourselves, and be of service, too. There's a way to carry the attitude of service into everything we do.

I hate being vulnerable. It means that sometimes people will take advantage of me, before I catch on to what's taking place. It means that sometimes I have to stand still and just eat the pain. It means that sometimes life really sucks but we still keep our hearts open, care, and keep giving, because that's the value we've acquired.

Ordinary people are capable of horrendous deeds. But God can also use ordinary people with just the smallest amount of pure desire in their hearts to accomplish tremendous works of service and good, too. I have to pray to keep my heart open, because closing it is the natural thing to do in this world. There's so much gravity out there—so many people that do so many things that cause everyone pain. I have to pray to be loving. I have to pray to be kind.

Those things don't come naturally to me. But they're still choices
we can each make.

"We've got to keep holding the door open for others, Melody,"
my friend Dan Cain said one day. "We wouldn't be here if someone
hadn't held it open for us.

"It's all gravy," he said.

———

Now let's go see what we can learn from
holy mountain number three.

OPPOSITES ATTRACT

Have you ever seen or played with the toy called Chinese hand-cuffs?

A Chinese handcuff, or finger trap, is a small, bamboo tube about five inches long. The idea is that you put an index finger in each end of the tube. Then the game begins. It's based on instinct. What do we do? We instinctively try to pull our fingers apart. What happens next is that we can't. The bamboo stretches and tightens when we try to pull our fingers apart, locking us in. A small paper toy has us trapped.

The harder we pull, the tighter it traps us.

Most people begin to panic then. Instead of thinking about what we're doing, we continue to do what our instincts led us to do in the first place—we keep trying to pull our fingers apart, then keep pulling harder—even though that doesn't work.

The Chinese handcuffs don't hold us hostage. We trap our-selves. Then emotions and the survival instinct keep us stuck until we unlock our brain and choose something else.

Just relaxing and letting go isn't enough to set us free. We've got to take action—do the opposite of what our baser instincts tell us to do. We've got to push our index fingers back toward the center, then gently, without pulling or forcing, ease out our fingers until we're free.

Once we learn the trick, it's no longer a trap. We bypass our instincts, panic, and emotions and make the right choice.

Whenever I get trapped by my reactions to life, my friend Michael helps me break free with this simple idea: "Just remember the old Chinese handcuffs trick. Relax and do the opposite of what you think."

Wutai Shan, holy mountain number three, was a circle of five peaks surrounding the monastic village of Taihuai.

"We could stay here for a month or so. Hike to each peak," Joe said. "Climb them all?"

I shook my head.

"Nope. Let's get a Jeep. Sometimes it's good to go the hard way. But it's okay to take advantage of technology, too," I said. We had a brief *discussion*. Then we traveled by Jeep to the top of each mountain. Atop the peaks, it was thirty below. The wind chill cut through our clothing. The blizzard made it nearly impossible to see. I was hypoxic—light-headed, exhilarated, breathless—from the altitude of these peaks. The temples were beautiful, but the novelty of monasteries was wearing thin. How many had we visited? Ten, twenty, maybe more?

To visit every monastery in the area, a person would have to be either a sincerely devout Buddhist or temple-crazed, the guidebook suggested. I didn't consider myself either.

"I'm getting templed out," I said to Joe.

He agreed.

Instead of visiting any more monasteries, we spent a day outside—walking, strolling, taking in the beauty of the terrain. I watched an old man harvesting wheat in a field. Then I took off my shoes and waded through a stream.

I was surprised at how I immediately came back into balance. The diminishing feeling of spirituality I was getting from the temple visits felt restored by being outside and absorbing nature. I felt the presence of God there.

That's it, I thought. *It's the yin yang circle. The circle of life (dark on one side, light on the other) keeps spilling from side to side. If you do anything too much—to excess—you'll wear it out. You'll be pushed into the other side until balance is achieved.*

"I have a problem with dualities," a friend said to me one day. "It's like, the second I feel happy, I feel scared because I know the happiness isn't going to last."

I wanted to explain to her what I had learned. I didn't. It's a complicated thing, and I'm not an expert on the mysteries of life. Besides, I don't like lecturing people. I enjoy watching them learn things for themselves. But this is part of what makes sense to me. Day and night are opposites, but they're part of the same thing— one twenty-four-hour cycle of life. It takes one to define the other, to give the other meaning, shape, and form.

Years ago, a woman pulled me aside. "You're going to learn about joy," she said. "I can feel it in my bones. It's time." I felt so excited, mentally calculating all the wonderful goodies that were coming my way. Did that mean a great love, a wonderful romance? Unbridled success? Relief from family tensions? A lot of good-hair days?

One week later, my son, Shane, died. I was heartbroken, devastated, all messed up, deep into my grief. I was furious about what this woman had said. What a cruel thing to do—a mean, nasty little trick by the universe. Have someone come into my life, someone I trusted, who looked into my eyes and told me I was going to learn about joy. *What a setup,* I thought. *The setup before the fall.*

On the eleventh anniversary of Shane's death, I recalled this conversation. I wasn't angry anymore about what this woman said. I laughed. She was right. The lessons usually don't come the way we think. The universe often hands us the opposite of what we're going to learn.

It sends us a situation where we want to attach ourselves and hold on tightly to learn about letting go and nonattachment. It may send us a situation of betrayal, one that hurts and enrages us, to teach us to forgive. The yin yang circle is a pretty good way to teach us things, once we learn how it works. Once we get the hang of it, it's not nearly as complicated as it appears.

The circle works with our behaviors, too. If we work too much, we're going to burn out, need to rest and play. If we give to others too much, we'll need to give to ourselves and learn to receive. It's a technique we can apply to remedy difficult situations. If someone is angry and upset, our natural reaction is to get angry, too. That usually doesn't remedy the situation, though. It keeps both people in the dark, angry side of life. What calms things is us moving the circle ourselves by bringing gentleness into play.

The purpose of the yin yang circle isn't to have us floundering around in either extreme, although that's frequently where many of us need to go. A friend explained it this way, after listening to her minister give a sermon at church:

"Sometimes if a piece of metal is bent way over to one side, you need to bend it way back in the other direction in order to get it to stand up straight."

The Middle Way—balance, moderation—is the goal.

Either we can wait until the circle dumps us—forces us—into the other side. Or we can achieve balance by deliberately moving there on our own.

Before we left Taihuai, Joe and I climbed a flight of steps that led to a temple in the middle of the village, in the middle of the circle of peaks. A tiny nun bowed to me, hands folded in front of her heart.

"Say *amitofa*," she said.

"What?" I asked.

She smiled and scurried away.

I asked every English-speaking person I met and many non-English-speaking people in China and Tibet about the meaning of that word. People recognized it. They liked it. "Oh, Yes. *Amitofa*," they happily said. But no one could explain it to me. For months after I came home, I searched for the meaning of the word. I finally met on-line, on the World Wide Web, a man who used and recognized the word. He had taught martial arts in Ireland and the United Kingdom and had spent years in China developing his skills.

"The closest meanings we have in English are "blessings" and "endless light."

That's it, I thought. Amitofa *means "by the Grace of God."*

Sometimes we can find balance and the Middle Way on our own. Sometimes to do that we need a little—or a lot—of help.

There's an old saying floating around. Some say it originated with Earnie Larsen in the Midwest: Insanity is doing the same thing over and over, expecting a different result. That's true, but for many of us it runs deeper than that. Insanity is feeling like we can't choose, or can't choose anything but the one thing that doesn't work.

In this section, we'll look at some situations where using the Chinese handcuffs trick helped people achieve balance—the Middle Way—in their lives. The secret is learning to substitute another word for *happiness*.

That word is *peace*.

1

She Found the Right Words

———

Thinking. Buzzing. She had so many words in her mind, but she couldn't catch a thought. She couldn't hold on to a word. Sherry's mind was running too fast. It was the middle of the night. She couldn't sleep. Her husband was lying next to her, asleep. Sherry got up, checked on her daughter in the next bedroom. She was sound asleep, too. Sherry locked herself in the bathroom, dug through her purse, got out the little plastic baggy, and sniffed another line of coke.

Her husband was a successful architect. He thought she was a cute little mom and a good wife. What he didn't know was hurting her, him, and their daughter, too. Sherry didn't like to use the word *addicted*. But it was getting harder and harder to deny that things were a little out of control.

He left for work that morning. She hadn't slept at all. Her daughter woke up. Sherry fixed her a bowl of cereal, then dug in her purse for more coke. It was gone. She was out.

Good, Sherry thought. *I need to stop. I need to quit.*

By midafternoon she was snorting more coke.

Another sleepless night ensued, with too many words and too many thoughts running wildly through her mind. *I can't get a grip,* Sherry thought. *I don't know what's going on.*

The next afternoon, after two sleepless nights, she stopped by a small bookstore in town. It wasn't a big chain—just a hole in the wall that sold recovery books and spiritual things. Sherry's daughter sat and played with some of the toys and books in the children's section. Sherry paced back and forth in the store. Finally she walked over to the manager.

"Yes?" the man said.

Sherry stood there, speechless, trying to catch the right thought, the right words. The manager looked at her. She looked at him.

"I need some help. I'm whacked out on coke. Please, help me do the right thing."

As clumsy and awkward as it felt, Sherry found the right words.

It can be easy to see someone else's addiction and their obvious need to ask for help. It's usually harder to see when we're the one trapped, stuck, doing the same thing over and over even though it doesn't work and we can't seem to stop doing that thing. We might be stuck with any type of problem—sexual acting out, financial problems, gambling, hurting someone else, or letting them hurt us.

The problem may be a quieter one such as depression, codependency, or anxiety. It might be a problem we're trying to unravel at work, in a relationship, or anyplace in our lives. If whatever we're doing to solve the problem doesn't solve the problem and we keep doing it anyway, we can relax, stop trying whatever it is that doesn't work, and try a new approach: open our mouths and ask for help.

We can ask a person, God, or both. And we may have to ask

more than once or more than one person to find the help we seek. Remember, once we make a choice, a powerful force sets in and guides us along the way. It's important to learn to give. But part of that circle of life also means choosing to ask for and receive help for ourselves.

One of the biggest tricks we play on ourselves is to convince ourselves that the way to win is to exert more power, exert more will, do it on our own. But sometimes the only way to win is to first admit defeat.

————————

Sometimes the real solution to our problem feels like the hardest thing to do, the opposite of what we think we should do, and the least likely winning approach. We simply admit the truth to others and ourselves: I can't solve this problem on my own, and I need some help.

2

Horse Sense

———

"If you want a horse to follow you around for life, approach it. Pet it," Jeanie's horseback-riding instructor said. "Tell the horse how wonderful it is. Give it a lot of strokes in a short amount of time. Then just turn around and walk away. Leave. Forget it. Let it go. That horse will be yours for life."

Jeanie finished her riding lesson. Cleaned the stable for a while. Then she got into her Jeep and drove home.

Something about what her instructor said haunted her all week.

I need people in my life so much—too much at times, Jeanie thought. *But instead of bringing people closer, my neediness drives them away.*

That's it, Jeanie thought. *My riding instructor just taught me the key to unlocking this whole enmeshment/abandonment thing.*

This particular circle of life can be an ugly, torturous, and confusing ordeal. We want more love and intimacy in our lives. We want to be closer to people. But the minute they or we step up to the plate, someone feels suffocated, disinterested. Enmeshed.

Many of us have done this dance in our relationships. He (or she) was interested, hot to trot, an avid and arduous pursuer in the beginning. You were reluctant. Disinterested. Unavailable. He won you over. The minute you got in, he was out.

Then you began obsessing and chasing him.

Or maybe it plays out a different way. We really want to be closer to people. We need to be in a relationship (sometimes with anyone) because we feel so abandoned inside. But when we're around people, our neediness drives them away.

Not all relationships are meant to work out. Sometimes it's better that he or she runs. But we can still start practicing the Chinese handcuffs trick in our encounters. It's a good—maybe great—relationship skill.

Resist that urge to smother and cling. Relax. Let go. Be genuinely interested in other people—not for what they can give you. Then, before you think it's time to hang up that phone or walk away, excuse yourself and leave. Get on with your life.

It may feel unnatural and awkward at first. But maybe it's time to turn the tables (or move to the other side of the circle).

Let them want more of you.

Letting go with love is a choice.

3

She Turned the Tables

Carolyn combed her hair, dabbed on some makeup, adjusted her skirt.

The doorbell rang. She let him in. She was so excited about their date.

He said hi, spotted his shirt hanging on the dining room chair, picked it up, then walked to the door.

Carolyn felt the anxiety and craziness brewing inside. *What's going on? I thought we were going to have some quality time together. Where's he going?* She looked at him with doe eyes, trying to hide the neediness she felt.

"Sorry," he said. "Something came up. I've got to leave."

Men are such jerks, Carolyn thought, watching him walk out the door.

Carolyn was pretty. Intelligent. Successful. But when she looked in the mirror, she didn't see that. She saw a needy kid wanting love. Each time she interacted with people and they left for any reason— whether it was to go to the store, go out by themselves for an evening, or just go on with their lives—she couldn't just say, *whatever,* and get on with her life.

Her mother had left when she was eight. Walked out, abandoned her. Then her dad had died when she was a young adult. Now each interaction with a human being left her feeling left.

She had applied the rules of therapy to these interactions, or at least she had applied what she thought were the rules. "I feel abandoned when you leave me like this," she'd tell her lover, her daughter, her friend. "And I feel hurt."

Sharing like this didn't get her what she wanted, however. Whenever she told someone how abandoned she felt by them, it made that person run.

Carolyn was visiting with a friend one evening, talking about how much she'd like to adopt a child someday. She talked about how angry and hurt she was with her mother for leaving her when she was a child.

"Maybe what you need to do first," her friend said, "is have a ceremony and adopt yourself."

Her friend's suggestion made sense. Carolyn had been looking for people to give her something she hadn't gotten as a child but could now give to herself. She made a list of all the things she wanted another person to do for her. Then she made another list that spelled out clearly how she could do these things for herself.

"Once I took responsibility for these needs lingering from childhood, I could be open, loving, and for God's sake at least let people go to the grocery store."

"Let me come by and take you for a ride in my Bentley."

"How about coming to the *Queen Mary* with me?"

"There's a party in town Saturday night. Would you like to accompany me?"

"I can't stop thinking about you. I can feel you, smell the scent of your hair, even though we're two thousand miles away."

Carolyn laughed. Four men wanting to date her at one time. Who would have thought? And who would have thought men could be as romantic as she'd discovered they are.

Sometimes doing the opposite of what we think gets us exactly what we want. When we don't have to be with someone to fulfill unmet needs from our past or use them as a stopgap measure for our grief, a pleasant event can transpire.

———————

After all those years of waiting to be chosen,
we finally get to choose.

4

He Knew How He Felt

Hank cooked dinner, set the table. Went all out and lit candles, too. He opened the door and let her in when the doorbell rang. Kissed her cheek. She acted a little odd, but women did that sometimes. He knew he hadn't seen her much lately; he'd been busy with work. But Hank was a romantic at heart.

And tonight he had plans.

They ate dinner. Made small talk. He thought he was particularly charming; he was on. She finished eating. Wiped her face daintily with her napkin.

"The only reason I came over tonight is to tell you we're through," she said. Hank watched her put on her coat, grab her purse, and walk out the door.

Geez, he thought. *I just got dumped.*

Hank talked about what happened to his friends. He talked about how he felt, too. "It doesn't feel good," he said.

Hank knew exactly what he was feeling.

The only thing he didn't want to do was feel how he actually felt.

● ● ●

I was talking to a woman who sees a therapist every week. "What feelings come up in your sessions?" I asked. "We don't really talk much about feelings," she said. "We talk about ways to change behaviors, intellectual kinds of things." "But what do you feel during your sessions each week?" "Hmmm," she said. "I guess the main feeling I have is bored."

I was talking to a friend in another state. Her grandmother had just died. "The hardest thing about my grief was that while I was so immersed in my feelings, my intuition was gone," she said.

"I hate feeling feelings," I said.

"Yuck," she said. "So do I."

We can talk about them. We can use them to try to control others. We can let them control us. Or we can cut off that part of us that feels—and sometimes we need to do that as a protective device. When I first reconnected to my emotions after twenty-four years of living life numb, every little emotion I had was such a big deal. I didn't know what to do with them or about them. I spent more time reacting to them than anything else.

"I feel this way now. Oh, now I feel like this," I'd say, telling anyone willing to hear.

It was hard to go down lower than my head. I liked to talk about how I felt. I didn't like to actually feel. Much of the time I felt like an outside observer watching myself, and usually watching myself stay emotionally stuck.

When I interviewed Elisabeth Kübler-Ross, I asked her about emotions, particularly fear. "How do you learn that lesson?" I asked. "What do you do about fear?"

"That's easy," she said. "When you're afraid, go down in the basement and scream."

She explained that many of the problems people suffer from are either due to or complicated by childhood repression of emotions. When they were children they weren't allowed or able to just feel whatever they felt—whether it was hurt, scared, angry, afraid, or any of the colorful nuances and shades our emotions can take.

No, we don't let feelings dictate our behavior. But if we don't feel them, that's what they're likely to do. No, it's usually not helpful to beat others over their heads with what we feel. It doesn't release our feeling, and it usually just annoys them. Yes, it's sometimes helpful to share with someone how we feel—as part of the process of either resolving problems, being intimate, or getting through a tough time.

It's helpful for those of us who disconnected from our feelings to know that however we feel at any moment in time is a valid and valuable event and that others have felt that way, too.

And if for some reason we've gone numb, we may need professional help.

But for the most part, our feelings are our own personal deal.

The real irony is this: some of the happiest, most joy-filled people I know are people who have been through some of the worst pain in the world. I don't know exactly why that happens, although it's part of the opposites thing. But this is my guess: once we're no longer afraid to feel any feeling that comes our way, we really do become happy, joyous, and free.

Go ahead. Do the opposite of what you think. Take a risk. Come back into balance. Feel what you feel. Or at least be willing to try. Feeling all our emotions gives color and passion to life.

So often we think, *Well, I've got to control that emotion, figure out in my head what do next, which choice I should make.*

When we allow ourselves to feel that emotion we're
trying to escape, it can be like magic. We just naturally know
what to do next.

5

Let the Winds Blow

———

Lynne didn't feel it coming.

She didn't know where it came from. She had yet to figure that out. But suddenly it was there. Her throat felt tight. Her heart was beating fast. Her neck was stiff. She had a pain in her head. She didn't know how she felt and she couldn't get clear on what she thought.

Cripes, she thought. *Another anxiety attack.*

When they first started hitting—once she got sober—she didn't know how to manage them. Now she had learned what to do. She stopped whatever she was doing. It was useless to try to accomplish anything while this was taking place. It just perpetuated the cycle. When she couldn't get anything done, she felt more panicked. Worse.

She went and lay down on the couch.

"I just keep asking God to hold me," she said. "Then I lie there until I pass out or He does."

• • •

When those cold winds blow out of nowhere, there's not much we can do to stop them. Fighting them or pretending they're not blowing doesn't help. We don't *have* to stand there in the cold.

────────

Sometimes the best we can do is find a safe,
warm place to rest until the icy winds stop.

6

She Got Swept off Her Feet

Amy Lou nervously fixed her hair, then brushed it again. She turned to her best friend: "Do I look okay?"

Her friend said yes. Then she looked at her watch.

"C'mon, girl. Let's go. It's time."

The ceremony was taking place at a small local church. There must have been at least one hundred people waiting expectantly in the room. The music played—the traditional wedding march—as Amy Lou gracefully moved to the front. Her dress was beautiful, flowing, off-white. A tight bodice laced down to her waist, a creamy flowing skirt, high-laced satin boots.

The minister said something. Amy Lou's high anxiety blurred the words. She looked into his eyes. He was so cute, standing there. He had come on to her so fast and hard. And he had come at the right time in her life. She was so sick of bad boys, unavailable men, men who didn't treat her right.

This one had really stepped up to the plate. He had bought her a huge diamond, treated her to beautiful dinners, quiet evenings at home. He vowed to give her everything she wanted—family, security, belonging, and stability. No more games and weaseling around love.

Sure, he had faults. The only pictures he had in his house were of himself. He was boring, bordering on inadequate, in bed. But she was sick of letting passion and emotions rule romance. That hadn't worked. This time she was taking another approach.

"Do you take this man to be your lawfully wedded husband?"

"I do," Amy Lou said.

"I now pronounce you man and wife. You may kiss the bride."

Amy Lou kissed him. The crowd cheered. She walked back down the aisle holding her new husband's arm. She smiled, greeted people, accepted their good wishes and hugs. He looked at her, smiled, and whispered, "How does it feel to be my wife?" She hoped she didn't look like a deer caught in a car's headlamps, because suddenly that's how she felt.

Oh my God, she thought. *What have I done? I just said "I do," but I think I don't.*

Sometimes doing the opposite of what we think means something different from what we think it does. Love and romance are a choice. But we can find the Middle Way between our emotions and our head.

Most people call that place the heart.

Many people I know have blundered their way through the relationship, dating, romance, and marriage scene. We try something. *Oops!* That didn't work. But we learn something valuable along the way.

A friend called me. His fiancée had canceled the wedding hours before it was scheduled to take place.

"What I feel bad about isn't losing her," he said. "I feel bad that I'm not getting married. I've been trying so hard to put a family together since my divorce. There's a lesson here," he added. "And I'm going to get it yet."

Doing the opposite of what we think when it comes to love, dating, and romance may mean taking a deep breath and slowing down.

Being swept off our feet is fun, exciting, thrilling. *At last,* we think, *I've found love.* Watch out. Beware. When we get swept off our feet too fast, we may land on our butts.

No matter how embarrassed we feel, if we make a mistake we can get up again. Remember the old Chinese handcuffs trick?

———————

We don't have to let our mistakes keep us trapped.

7

Her Fantasy Became Real

Melanie checked her caller ID and her voice-mail messages.

He had left one message. But he had called six times.

Two years ago she would have given anything—anything in the world—to have this man calling her all the time. Now all it did was irritate her. Actually, it kind of made her sick.

She listened to the message. "Hi, it's me." *Why do they always call themselves "me," she thought. Why don't they say their name? How many "me"s do they think there are in this world? Or do they think they're the only one?*

He wanted to see her again tonight.

Ugh. She'd rather stay home.

He's so handsome. I've got to have him. He's everything I want. Please, God, just let me have him and I'll never ask for anything more. She had begged, pleaded, prayed, whined, moaned, and died inside for two years over this guy. Oh yeah. She'd been convinced it was true love. Soul mates. The real thing.

That was when she couldn't have him, when he dumped her and became involved with somebody else. But the more she couldn't have him, the more that nagging little seed had grown in her mind: *I've got to have him or this lifetime will be incomplete.*

She had let go. Gone on with her life. Actually, she'd had a good time when she moved on. Then he had broken up with his girl-friend. The tables had turned. Now he wanted her.

It was interesting at first, amusing. But the novelty had quickly worn off. *He's boring. A jerk. Self-centered. Dull. Manipulative. Untrust-worthy. He doesn't seem to like to take baths, and he's not very smart. What did I see in him that made me so fanatically obsessed and convinced we were in love? Am I just running away because I'm scared? Am I sabotaging myself?* Melanie pushed Delete, erased his message, then wondered how long she could stall before she returned his call.

It took Melanie six more weeks of miserable dates before she realized she had never been in love with this guy. She had fallen in love with her fantasy of who she thought he was.

The easy and natural thing to do when we make a mistake is to stop believing that we can trust ourselves. Doing the opposite of what we think doesn't mean we live from our heads. It means we stop listening to the obsessive voice within that screams at us and listen to that quiet inner voice instead.

Who knows? Maybe that relationship you call a mistake wasn't a mistake after all. What if it was exactly what you needed at the time?

Did you learn something? Did it help move you down your path? Did it help you come alive?

"I was in a disastrous relationship after my father died," a woman said to me. "I look back on it now and I'm horrified at the choice I made. But in retrospect, this is what I believe. I was walking around so numb and grief-stricken. Getting into—and out of—that relationship helped me come back to life."

Some people have a neat and tidy path when it comes to love.

Others have a more circular, jagged, rocky, uphill and downhill path.

Some relationships are for a season. Some relationships last for a life.

Who are you going to be with—friends, lovers, spouse? How long will you stay? What will you learn? How will you take that lesson into your other relationships? Guess what?

It's your choice.

———

Maybe that relationship that made you doubt yourself
so much came along to help you learn to listen to
and trust your inner voice.

8

He Went to Extremes

It was a first date, no big deal.

They went to a nice Italian restaurant for a tasty meal. She leaned across the table and whispered to him: "Want to blow this joint and go get high? I've got some ecstasy. We could have some fun?"

His heart beat harder and faster. He ran it through his mind. He'd never done ecstasy. He didn't even know what it contained. But it sounded intriguing, the word.

"What's in it?" he asked.

"Oh, I don't know," she said. "I think a little of everything. You know. Heroin. Cocaine. Meth."

It felt like a brick hit him on the head. What was he thinking of? He had been sober for nineteen years.

"You know what, hon—I'd really like to get high. I don't think you'll ever understand how much. But this is the thing. We live in a world of balance. I used up all my chemical highs this lifetime. I've been in a program of recovery for nineteen years. Now is my time to be chemically free."

She scowled.

"Don't you think you're being a bit fanatical?" she said. "Do you really believe that if you got high one time, you'd start drinking and using drugs again? Besides, I'll never tell anyone. No one would ever have to know but you and me."

He felt the temptation swinging round his way again. He went back inside his head. No one would ever know but her and him. Would he go back out again, have a relapse with alcohol and drugs from using just one time? Maybe. But maybe not.

"Besides," she said. "I'll stay with you for a few days, make sure you don't start using again."

This time her words snapped him back to reality. Like anyone in the world could keep him from getting high.

"I speak at a lot of meetings. I sponsor people—help them get straight, too. Maybe they'd never know. But I'd know what I did. This is the deal," he said, leaning across the table and talking in a low voice. "I didn't get myself sober. My compulsion to use drugs and alcohol was out of control. I lost my ability to choose. My sobriety is due to a thing we call Grace.

"As long as I've been given the ability to choose—which I didn't have for a long time—I think I'll choose to say no."

Like the happy little nun on the mountain told me, "*Amitofa*."

Enough said.

———

Gear up. Make sure you've got all your lessons in your
backpack. The biggest, tallest mountain yet looms ahead.
Watch out for the monkeys, though.
I've heard they bite.

GO FOR THE GOLD

"We don't see things as *they* are; we see things as *we* are," a friend said. "That's what scientists, Zen, Christianity—all the religions—now say."

There's an old story circulating in therapy circles. A therapist is conducting a group. And the group facilitator tells the client, "Go ahead. Tell the group everything you've done wrong, everything you're ashamed of, everything you feel guilty about. Everyone in here has done as much—or more—wrong than you."

So the client spills his guts. Bares the secrets of his soul.

Then he sits there waiting.

The group leader and all the other members of the group sit looking at him, horrified.

"Oh, how awful," they say. "We've never done that!"

Well, a lot of the time we walk around life feeling like that client. And feeling this way changes how we see everything: the world, events, other people, ourselves, and God.

Some people say it's love that makes the world go round. That may be. But when I get to spinning in circles in my life, it's usually because of guilt.

Three routes lead to the top of Emei Shan, holy mountain number four. One is a long hard path that winds through the monkey forest in the valley, then ascends to the top. The other is a long hard route, too, but this one ascends more directly. The third is fast and easy—cable cars all the way.

Joe and I decided to do a combination of routes: We'd take the path through the valley on the way up; we'd take the other path down. This climb would take three or four days.

We headed into the monkey forest in the valley. After hiking for seven hours, we hadn't seen any monkeys and it was starting to get dark. But we found ourselves in a lush, magical place. The air was filled with water sounds, from the river rushing through the bottom and the waterfalls on either side. Bamboo platforms lined the hillsides. Old swinging bridges draped across the river, big enough for one person at a time—or several monkeys—to scurry across.

Valleys can be beautiful places, too, I thought.

We unrolled our sleeping bags and set up camp on one of the bamboo platforms built into the side of the hill. We were violating the rules by camping there, and we both felt a little nervous as we lay under the night sky staring at the stars.

"What's that?" I asked Joe, pointing to a light in the distance.

"Dang. We're busted. That's a guard waving a flashlight," he said.

We both lay quietly, wondering what to do next. We watched the light bounce back and forth. It didn't seem to be coming any closer.

"Maybe we'll be okay," I whispered.

As soon as I said it, six more lights came on. We watched the lights approach, then back off. I wondered what they'd do to us when and if we were caught. Kick us out? To where? It was a five- to seven-hour hike to anywhere from here. Arrest us?

"Those aren't guards," I finally whispered to Joe.

"What are they? Monkeys with headlamps?"

"They're the biggest fireflies I've ever seen," I said.

The next morning we were up at dawn. We hiked through the valley, across plateaus, then began the ascension to the top. We made it to a monastery by the end of the second day and decided to sleep there. We were still at least one day away from the top.

Steps. Steps. And more steps. I was cold and tired. I had been in China for five weeks. I wanted my own bed. Home. The novelty of this quest was beginning to wear thin.

There was hot water but no tea in my room. I went to a snack stand behind the monastery and tried to buy some tea. The man running the stand instead tried to sell me a soda—for at least double the price it should have been. I refused. I walked to the next stand. The woman who ran this shop was round and short. She had a big smile on her face and a baseball cap on her head.

"I want to buy some tea to bring to my room," I said.

She dug through her supplies, then stuck a bag of tea in my hand. "No charge," she said. "Enjoy."

The next morning, I woke up. I wanted a cup of coffee to start my day. I went back to the stand where I had gotten my tea.

"Six o'clock. Seven o'clock. Sun up. Good morning!" the round smiling woman with the baseball cap said. I ordered breakfast—rice and coffee. I watched the dour little man running the stand next to hers. Nobody was coming there to eat breakfast. They were all piling into her café.

Joe and I headed to the top of the mountain after breakfast. Mount Emei was the highest and hardest of all—so far. After walking up steps for six hours, we decided to catch the cable car the rest of the way to the top.

The altitude was so high at the top of this mountain I could barely walk.

I sat on a ledge, watching people crowd into the temple at the top.

Some were postulating and praying. Whether they walked or took the cable cars, they had come to pray and find the spiritual value of this place. Others were there sightseeing.

So often in life I've gotten religious values confused. I thought being a spiritual person meant preaching and espousing spiritual truths. Yet the moments when I've felt closest to God and people were the times when I told them something I was feeling or had done—something that made me feel odd, weird, not good enough, like an outcast—and they said, "Yeah, I've felt or done that, too."

The only way to get to the tiptop of Mount Emei was by monorail. Joe and I rode the little train, then walked up more steps. I was so hypoxic from the altitude I was stumbling up the steps, almost crawling, by then. We made it. At the very top was a bell. *Dong. Dong. Dong.* We took turns ringing it and wrote our names in a book.

We sat there for a while, then walked around and looked at the sights. The view from the top was spectacular—much different from what we had seen in the valley. Being at the top of the mountain is fun but how long can you stay there? Both the valleys and the peaks are places we pass through.

We headed back down to the monastery we had stayed at the night before.

Before the cable car arrived that would return us to our place on the steps, a few hours away, I went shopping at some of the stands. One stand offered a selection of herbs and teas. I purchased a bag of exotic tea. I was hoping I had finally found this mysterious *altitude sickness tea* I had heard about before the trip.

When we arrived back at the monastery that night, I looked at the tea I had just purchased and had a little battle with myself. *Mine, mine, mine*, I thought. *No*, I thought. *I owe it to her.*

I walked to the stand of the woman who had given me tea yesterday. I pressed the bag of tea into her hand and thanked her for her kindness.

She accepted my gift.

Is that what this mountain is about? I wondered. *What comes around goes around and comes back to us? Karma—the ultimate game of cause and effect?*

The next day we headed back down the final stretch of that mountain. The remaining trip down was long, tiring, and strenuous. The sign said 1.4 kilometers to the bottom. But we'd been walking longer than that. Then it occurred to me: someone had messed with the sign. It should have read 14 kilometers instead.

"How much longer to the end, do you think?" I kept pestering Joe.

"Don't start, Melody," he said. "We'll know when the climb is done because we'll be standing in the parking lot where we began. Just keep putting one foot in front of the other until then."

"I used to really believe in the Golden Rule when I was a kid," a friend said. "But I got so sick of watching the bad guys win—and me lose—that I guess I pretty much gave up. The real name of the game out there seems to be What's in It for Me."

I've found the oddest thing happens throughout my life when I've practiced the Golden Rule. When I give to most people—whether it's love, compassion, forgiveness, or money—the person I give to doesn't necessarily give back to me.

Usually they want more.

Once in a while someone steps up to the plate at work, in romance, in our family—or maybe a friend comes along—and that person really does care. They stand by us through our good and bad times. They forgive us when we screw up. Most important, they believe in us. When they say things like *You'll get through this; I believe in you; You're not that bad, kid; I've done the same thing; Look at all the good you've done*—they mean it. And for that moment we genuinely experience unconditional love.

They're really sorry (not secretly happy) when something bad happens to us. And when they give to us, it's not because they're hoping to get something back.

That's what the lesson here is really about, I thought much later, after I got back to the United States. *It's about forgiveness, mercy, compassion, and love.*

In this section we'll look at stories about how these virtues played a part in the choices some people have made. It's easy to start thinking we're the only ones walking around feeling guilty and insecure. People look so confident and self-assured on the outside. The best-kept secret in town is how we really feel inside our skin.

Forget about the brass ring.

Go for the real gold.

Slow down. It's lower than your head. That's it. Get into your heart. Did you really think you were the only one who felt and thought that way?

See how that spiral of guilt turns into a circle of love.

1

She Called the Law

———

Sophie stood in her friend's kitchen. Last weekend's events had been too much. Maybe if she explained it to someone else, she could understand it herself.

"I cannot believe what happened," Sophie said, shaking her head.

"You know that Richard and I broke up months ago, right? Well, I had a man friend over to my apartment Saturday night. We went on a date. We went to a party together; it was fun. He came up to my apartment afterward. We visited for a while, then I walked him down to his car. His windshield was shattered. Someone had thrown a rock through it.

"I know who that someone was.

"Richard has harassed me ever since we broke up; he's having a hard time *letting go*. He thinks I belong to him and we'll get back together someday. And he gets upset when I see anyone else."

"What did you do?" her friend asked.

"I called the police, put in a report," Sophie said. "I did what I needed to take care of myself. But the police said it's hard to get fingerprints off a rock.

"That's not the best part, though," Sophie said. "Get this. I went to church Sunday morning. Richard sings in the choir. He was just standing there shouting and singing 'Hallelujah, Praise the Lord.'

"He even had tears streaming down his face."

Sophie just kept shaking her head. "It'd be funny if it wasn't so sad.

"One of Richard's neighbors called me last night. She invited me to a party at her house; I knew her from the time Richard and I were together. I said no, I didn't think I'd be going. Then she asked me where Richard has been. She said she hasn't seen his car parked in front of his house.

"I know what's going on," Sophie said. "He's hiding his car because he's afraid that what he did to someone else is going to happen to him."

———————

If the law of karma doesn't get us, our own guilt will.

2

She Blamed Herself

Tina listened to the news broadcast on the drive to work. "And the State Department of Transportation is reporting that it will take approximately one year to repair the damage to the highway. . . ."

A year? Tina thought. *A year?*

That highway was the main road into town. Most of her customers came from the next city over, a larger city than where she lived. Rent. Employee salaries. How was she going to manage? Her business was going broke.

She slowed down, as she usually did, when she passed a particular street. God, she wished she lived there. But it was too expensive under the best of circumstances. Now that her business was inevitably going to close, she wouldn't be able to afford a house there for sure.

She loved her business. She was losing that. She hated the condo where she lived. It looked like she'd be stuck there.

Everything was going wrong.

It must be something I've done, Tina thought. She calculated all the things she felt guilty about. A couple of ghosts from her past popped immediately to mind. She had tried to make amends the best that she could. But the longer she lived, the more mistakes she made.

Tina opened the shop and spent some time looking at the records and the money in her bank account. She couldn't afford to keep the business going. She wasn't a quitter, but some simple math made that decision clear.

She was going to have to break the news to her employees soon. It wasn't fair not to give them notice so they could begin looking for new jobs. They'd be upset. They had a right to be. She felt guilty for depriving them of their jobs. But she was upset, too. She had sunk $100,000 into this business, and every month it kept sucking her bank account dry.

It's not just the money, Tina thought. *That business was my dream. I didn't want it just for myself. I was so hoping it could serve people in the surrounding communities, do a good deed for them, too.*

She broke the news to her employees late that afternoon. That week they started a going-out-of-business sale. She watched the money dribble in from selling the last of her inventory. Before long, her stock was almost gone.

"Can I talk to you?" a woman asked one day.

Tina figured she was probably going to try to get her prices down lower than they already were.

"Sure," Tina said. "Talk away."

"I've had a change in my circumstances," the woman said. "I probably should have seen it coming. But I guess we never do. Anyway, I've got to sell my home and sell it quickly. And for some reason, I felt I should talk to you."

She told Tina the address of the home. It was on the street where Tina dreamed about living. She told Tina the price. That's when Tina got turned off, leery and skeptical. The price made the home a steal! Tina could afford that. Anyone could.

This is too good to be true, Tina thought. *I'm not going to waste my time.*

The woman badgered Tina about coming to look at the home. Tina hemmed and hawed. Said no at first. Later that day, she talked to a friend.

"Why don't you at least stay open. Go check it out," he said. "I'll come with you if you'd like."

Tina reluctantly agreed. She knew in her mind what she wanted in a home. She was already living in a place that wasn't right for her; she didn't want to commit to—buy—one that wasn't what she wanted. She'd rather stay where she was.

The next day Tina drove to the address. She looked at the exterior. *Just what I expected,* Tina thought. *It looks awful. I bet it's a dump.*

"Just go in and look," her friend urged.

Tina went to the door. "If it's not right, I'm walking out instantly," she said.

She knocked. The woman opened the door. Tina went in and sat down. This home was beautiful inside. She looked upstairs and down. It contained everything—every single thing—on her wish list.

"I thought I was being paid back because of everything I had done wrong in my life," Tina said later to a friend. "I almost missed that opportunity because of my own guilt and prejudgments. I assumed that the bad things happening in my life—the losses— were punishment for wrongs I had done. And I assumed that any good that happened was too good to be true."

"I feel guilty about that," I said to a friend one day, explaining my reaction to something I had said or done. It may have been some- thing stupid, some little thing. Or something I did as part of taking care of myself.

"No, you don't feel guilty about *that*," my friend said. "*You feel guilty about everything.*"

He was right. Sometimes I even feel guilty for having so much guilt.

We search. We question. We feel. We wonder. We review our pasts. We try to do better and be better. Most of us really want to get this thing right. A lot of things have gone wrong. Sometimes the things that went wrong started early—like when we were still in our mother's womb.

"The first thing I remember my mother saying isn't *I love you*," a man said. "It's *I wish you'd never been born.*"

Could it be that all that guilt we're feeling isn't really our own? Hmm. That's an idea.

"My dad is an alcoholic. Still drinking. When he calls me he doesn't tell me he loves me. He asks if I still love him. Get this," a woman I know said. "I feel guilty because *he* drank and didn't love *me* enough.

"Sometimes it's like I have a big open sore. *Don't ask me if I love you*, I say. *Tell me that you love me.*

"Then I feel guilty about that."

Sometimes we need to make amends for things we've done. Sometimes we don't because all we've done is batted things about in our head. The best antidote I've seen for this kind of guilt was demonstrated in a scene in the movie *The Royal Tenenbaums*.

The ne'er-do-well father in this J. D. Salinger–type story, played by Gene Hackman, had done a lot of things wrong in his life—left his family for another woman, been manipulative, that whole deal. Now he had come back to his family. In his own screwy way he was trying to set things right.

"You ought to be ashamed of yourself," his daughter said while they were out walking together one day.

He thought about what she said. "Well, I am," he said. Then he immediately continued with what he'd been trying to do and say.

The point is, sure we feel guilty. Some of it's our own. Some isn't. It comes and goes in burbles. Most people with an active conscience have a lot of thoughts they think. Sometimes it's easier to think about things than to feel how much things hurt.

Wrestle with your demons. Talk to your angels. You may not be as far off as you think you are. Sometimes what we need to do when we're feeling guilty is change our behavior, make amends. But sometimes all we need to do when we're feeling guilty is say, *Yup, it's back. I'm feeling guilty again.*

Then go on with our life.

The real irony of these gnarly little burbles of guilt, fear, and self-contempt is that once I've gone on with my life—taken a walk, watched a movie, done something gentle and loving and nice—I often look back on the very thing I did that I felt guilty about and say, *Wow, that's exactly what I was supposed to do.* Or I think, *What was I making such a ruckus about? That was no big deal.* Or I look at it and say to myself, *That wasn't as bad as I thought it was. A lot of people have done that.*

---

*Whew. Despite what we've convinced ourselves of,
maybe we're not such odd ducks after all. When we look
around and everything we see looks like our fault, maybe
it's time to take a break from our guilt until we can
see with the eyes of our hearts.*

3

He Got Even

At first Carl was numb. Then he felt hurt.

Then all he wanted was revenge.

Mark was his friend. His business partner. Carl had trusted him. And Mark had just ripped him off for seventy grand.

How could he do it? How could he show up at work each day and look me in the eye? Carl wondered. *What a phony. What a fraud. What a jerk. Now he's walking around town all smug, and I'm standing here with no recourse and I'm out all that money.*

Plus, Carl thought, *I just lost a friend.*

No, I didn't, Carl thought, arguing with himself. *That guy was never a friend. Friends don't do that to each other. He was using me from the start.*

I'm going to get him, Carl thought, *if it's the last thing I do.*

Carl loaded all his books and records into the car and marched to the police station. He dragged his box of papers inside and asked to talk to whoever could help him press charges. He didn't care what had gone on in the past between him and Mark. Mark had ripped him off. He had committed a felony. Carl was going to put him in jail.

The lieutenant on duty listened to the story. He looked at the stack of papers Carl had brought in.

"It sounds like a felony was committed," the officer said. "But the burden of proof still rests with you. Somehow you're going to have to prove that your partner wasn't entitled to that money. Because you and your partner had equal rights to that bank account, it's going to come down to your word against his."

"What are you saying?" Carl asked.

"I'm saying that if what you're saying is true, you had money stolen from you. But proving it and getting a conviction against your partner is another issue. And it's by no means guaranteed. I'm not certain the D.A. will pick up the case without more proof than you have."

Carl thanked the officer, took his papers, and went home. In his mind he went through every option.

He could file a civil suit. But that could drag on for years, and cost more money than what Carl had lost.

"Do you want me to have some people go rough him up?" one of Carl's friends asked. "Yeah, I'd like that," Carl said. "But it goes against my values. No matter how angry I am, I don't believe in violence.

"But it's tempting," Carl said. "It sure would feel good."

Carl stewed for weeks. Then he came up with a plan. If he couldn't put him in jail and wouldn't hurt him physically, at least he could hurt his reputation in town. He could fix it so Mark would lose all his friends, because everyone—everyone—was going to know who he was and what he had done.

With vengeance in mind, Carl began telling anyone who even remotely knew Mark what Mark had done. People listened and expressed a slight amount of sympathy. But Carl was seeing something different in their eyes from what he had hoped for and planned. Instead of agreeing with him about what a bad person Mark was, people were looking at Carl—raging, stewing, and venting so wildly—like he—Carl—was nuts.

"I could feel myself talking and acting insanely," Carl said. "I could feel that I was out of control with my rage. I just didn't know what else to do. I felt so mad, so hurt, so impotent in this situation. I had been betrayed. It felt wrong that Mark could just waltz away scot-free with no consequences after what he did to me.

"He had some karma coming from this," Carl said. "And I was going to make sure he got it. If I couldn't put him in jail, at least I could let everyone know what he had done. I had to do something—anything—to get some relief."

The problem was, Carl's vendetta didn't help him feel better.

Whenever he raged to someone about what Mark had done, Carl felt worse. He felt even more angry and upset than he had felt before. So far the only thing his vendetta was accomplishing was keeping him—Carl—upset.

"Of course I was angry, hurt, and upset," Carl said. "But what I was doing didn't work. It was time to try something else. It was so hard at first. But I kept forcing myself to do it anyway. This is what I did. I started praying for my ex-friend and partner, Mark. Each time his name came to mind, I asked God to bless him. Oh, I didn't mean it at first. Didn't mean it at all. But it was better than what I had been doing. Because even if I didn't mean it, I stopped feeling so irritated and upset."

"Probably ten, twenty, or thirty times a day, Carl's name and my anger and resentment popped into my mind. Each time they did, I thought or said out loud, *God bless him. God bless him.* It took months of doing this, but slowly my anger began to turn around."

Now, when Carl thinks of Mark or hears his name, he doesn't

feel angry or upset. Sometimes he feels sad, thinking of the days of friendship and partnership that are gone.

"I don't want him back in my life again. Too much water has passed under that bridge," Carl says. "But I truly wish him well. I wish him happiness, blessings, and success. We all make mistakes. We do things. We get desperate. I hope his life is good."

Carl got even, but not like he thought. Within nine months of forgiving Mark, Carl got a business contract that brought in unexpected profits of more than five times what Mark had stolen from him.

More than that, Carl got even with himself again.

He was restored to peace.

Wouldn't it be nice if life, karma, and the Golden Rule worked like a bubble-gum machine? All we had to do was put a quarter of love in, and we got one or two pieces of love instantly back?

Most of the time practicing the Golden Rule feels more like playing a slot machine. You put your money in and you may or may not get something back. We all like those situations where it's easy to give love and practice our virtues. And where as soon as we give, we instantly receive. But the world doesn't usually work that way—at least it hasn't in my life.

The places where I am tested and challenged are always the places where I would least prefer to have anything go wrong. The situations are usually a surprise, not what I expected at all, and definitely not the circumstances I would have chosen if I could have selected the test.

Resentment and revenge often look like the only reasonable response.

Sometimes we really take it on the chin. Let it all sink in. Yes, I know. It really hurts. But once we get through feeling mad, hurt, victimized, and upset, what are we going to do?

We can keep ourselves so busy being angry and hurt we don't see the gifts—or the way that life could send new blessings back to us.

———

Go ahead. Put another quarter of love in the machine. Who knows? This time you might get back your peace.

4

Mommy Dearest

The telephone rang. Jackie answered the call. It was her sister. She got right to the point:

"I'm just calling to let you know Mom died in her sleep last night."

Jackie startled awake. It was only a dream, but it haunted her. She got up. It was the middle of the night. She made herself a cup of tea. She couldn't shake the feelings she had about her dream.

Sadness. Guilt. Nostalgia. A wish for better, more in their relationship. Jackie had barely talked to her mother for years. Occasionally she would do a dutiful act. But her mom was a little sketchy. A little, hell. A lot of the time her mom was downright nuts.

How would I feel if my mom died right now? Jackie wondered throughout the next week. She flashed back to a time when she was small, five or six. Her mom had been so wonderful then—the only person in her world. *Well, maybe not wonderful*, Jackie thought. But she had loved her mom with the innocence of a child.

The older Jackie had grown, the more difficult their relationship had become. Now Jackie barely talked to her mom. And when she did, she closed herself off. She did what she had to do to survive—in her life and in that relationship. She had been to therapy. She had worked on herself. Her mom hadn't wanted to listen to any of her feelings; none of her discoveries about herself meant a hill of beans to her mom.

The bottom line is that if my mom died right now, Jackie thought, *the relationship would feel incomplete.*

"I spent so much time looking at what was negative about the relationship I never bothered to look at the gifts," Jackie said. "She taught me strength. She taught me persistence. She taught me if a job was worth doing it was worth doing well. By what she didn't give me—the holes in our relationship—I learned what I wanted to give to my kids. Most of all, by my anger with her and my gross disappointment in my family life, she's teaching me the most valuable lesson of all.

"She's given me an opportunity to learn what it means to forgive."

―――――――

Isn't it funny how when we forgive others,
the person we really let off the hook is ourselves?

5

Her Halo Fell Off

———

Samantha and her brand-new husband left church and went to the restaurant. It wasn't her first marriage; it wasn't his, either. He had wanted her to visit the church he attended. Afterward, they were meeting his ex-wife at a restaurant to talk about some *things*.

"I liked the church," Samantha said. "By the time we got to the restaurant, I was feeling all good and glowing inside. It felt like I was wearing a halo on my head."

Samantha ordered a piece of pie. Her husband excused himself to use the rest room. That was the moment the ex-wife chose to come strolling in.

"It felt awkward at first, just sitting there with each other, without him. But we had a friendly relationship—for the most part," Samantha said. "And she and my husband had two children together. We were going to be in each other's lives for a long time. I felt it was important that we have a good relationship and learn to get along."

One thing led to another. Samantha's husband came back to the table.

"The three of us began talking about issues we were having about visitation and such. But I knew it ran deeper than that," Samantha said. "I could feel it. She was upset that I had come along and changed the way things were."

It happened fast, as switches usually do. One moment her husband and the ex-wife were discussing things. The next the ex-wife had her finger in Samantha's face.

"You stay out of this," the ex-wife screamed. "This doesn't involve or concern you! You have no right to be involved. Just shut up!"

Samantha had felt her blood boiling ever since the discussion began. But the moment the ex-wife shook her finger in Samantha's face was the moment Samantha's halo fell off.

"I started screaming. Reacting. I stuck my finger right back in her face, shaking it and telling her never to do that again. My nails are long. I know I scratched her. It turned into a catfight, right there in public, in that restaurant. I couldn't believe what I was doing," Samantha said. "I don't like acting like that. Later I could see what happened. I lost it because I felt attacked."

Samantha excused herself, went to the rest room, and tried to regain her composure. By the time they left the restaurant, Samantha was back to her old self. She apologized for her behavior, saying she was really sorry for the way she acted and what she said.

"I might have been justified in what I did," Samantha said. "Some situations are really hard—especially when I feel attacked. But I don't like it when I behave like an animal. I don't particularly like this woman, but I want us to be at peace and I want to be at peace with myself."

We all have our moments.

Well, most of us do.

I was talking to a friend one evening about whether he thought a particular person I knew was going to betray my trust—or not. "I'd like to say absolutely not, but I can't," my friend said. "Under the right circumstances, we're all capable of doing almost anything in the world."

————————

*Maybe we should put a few more quarters into that
slot machine—you know, the one marked forgiveness.
Never can tell when we might get lucky and get a
few back for ourselves.*

6

He Wanted to Make Amends

———

He paced back and forth in his studio apartment, thinking back, trying to recall. Things had gotten so fuzzy over the years. Drinking had complicated his memory. At least he was sober now.

What was he thinking of? What were his motives? Their relationship had gotten so damn insane at times. *Maybe if I just call her and explain, tell her how sorry I really am, then she'll understand that although I hurt her, I never meant her any harm.*

It took him a couple days to work up the courage. Then he reached for the telephone.

"I know I've embarrassed you, hurt you, disappointed you. I'm sorry," he said.

He could feel her anger across the lines.

"When we got together, we both had so many issues," he said. "I think we both brought each other the worst of our post-traumatic stress disorder. I had my problems. And you were in a lot of pain. I wanted to stay sober. I really did. For some reason I kept ending up drunk. I don't know why so many people can get clean and stay clean. I've relapsed so many times."

He could feel her response. An angry "I know."

"But this is the thing. I had lost all my hope. Every time I'd try, I'd fail again. One more time. A lot of the time when I relapsed, I kept hoping I'd go to bed drunk and just die in my sleep. I didn't. Each morning, I woke up.

"I needed to find someone I thought had value, someone who had lost their hope, too. Then I ran into you. I thought if I helped you find your sense of meaning and purpose in life again, maybe I could find some purpose in mine."

He explained that he didn't need to see her again, didn't want anything from her, he just wanted to make amends. He wanted them to be at peace.

I listened carefully to his words.

Then I said, "Apology accepted," and I thanked him. Some people may call him—or me—codependent. I don't care.

After my son died, he's the guy that saved my life.

It's a pretty imperfect place, this world.

People don't love us the way we want. Things don't go as we hoped and planned. Sometimes it's easy to give up and lose hope. I know I've misplaced mine a couple of times.

I had just left yoga class one day with these instructions from the teacher: "I want you to practice compassion for people in other parts of the world."

That's a good idea, I thought as I was driving home. *Think compassion.* When I got home, there was a message from Tracey, a friend in another state. We had lost contact after I moved to California. I hadn't seen her for about seven years.

I had met her through her father. We had both worked at the same rehab center in Minnesota, trying to save other people's lives and, in the process, save our own. Those were the old days—when you'd go into a group for ten or twelve hours. And when you came out, you came out changed.

He had relapsed and ended up going back to prison.

He was an intelligent, clever guy.

There was the time back in the 1960s in a southern state when he bought a used cop car. It still had all the machinery intact. Whenever he needed money, he'd put on the siren and the red light, pull someone over, and give them a choice: they could go to court, or they could pay him on the spot.

Once he and a friend were at another friend's apartment. The couple they were visiting got into a domestic disturbance. A neighbor called the police. When the police arrived, they took everyone there to jail—the couple and both the men who were visiting them. My friend gave his testimony. Then he spotted a typewriter at the police station. He liked it. So he stole it—walked out with it—right in front of the policemen.

When he got back home, he discovered it didn't have a ribbon cartridge in it. He got upset, went back to the police station, worked his way into the supply cabinet, found a couple of cartridges, and stole them, too.

For a time he had his hands on a set of keys that unlocked the coin machines in Laundromats. When the Laundromat closed, he would break in, unlock the machines, and escape with all the coins. In those days it was a good score. He had the timing down. He knew how much time he'd have from the time he broke in the front door and triggered the alarm until the police arrived.

One night he miscalculated. The police car arrived while he was in front of the Laundromat getting ready to get away. He looked at the policeman. Kept his composure. "He was about five feet eleven inches. Thin. Dark hair. And he ran that way," he said, pointing toward the end of the block. The police pursued the mythical robber and my friend escaped.

He eventually got sober, then started counseling others. When he relapsed and went back to jail, his daughter got hurt and mad.

He was in prison for seven years. When he finally got out, he tried to reconnect with her. "Only if you're on your deathbed," she said.

It didn't take long for him to get there. Within three months he called her from the hospital. He had known he was sick, but he didn't want to die in jail.

That's when I met Tracey, his daughter. She asked me to sit at the hospital with her while we both waited for him to die. It was about three years after Shane died; I was no longer so afraid of death.

"I asked him once why he kept using when he knew using would kill him or put him in jail," Tracey said. "I asked him why he kept hurting himself and hurting me. He said he couldn't live with some of the choices he'd made.

"I knew vaguely what he was talking about—some dark awful secrets from his past. In an odd way, I understood," she said.

My friend believed he was forgiven by God. He told me that. But as clever, bold, and ingenious as my friend was, he could never figure out how to forgive himself.

Now, seven years later, Tracey was calling me because she wanted to talk to someone who she knew would understand. In the past year and a half, her daughter had come down with leukemia. After a remission, then a bone-marrow transplant, her thirteen-year-old daughter had just died.

"I didn't walk into the unknown," she said. "Life catapulted me there.

"I beat the odds. I got sober myself. Finished school. Got my degree. Got a good job. Got myself a nice place—moved out of the trailer park. I guess I kept thinking that life would get easier, that the lessons would stop.

"I'm so angry at God right now. I'm so mad," she said. "Sometimes I just kick at the air. But this is also what I believe. It's all just lessons. And each one gets harder because each one prepares us for the next."

We've all got a history of choices we've made. Some have worked out. Some haven't. Some of us have a little guilt. Some of us have a lot.

I've known people like my friend who couldn't figure out how to live with the choices they made. I've known other people who could. Remember Sherry, from the beginning of this book? She was the pregnant woman who got into an accident and gave birth to a seriously handicapped child as a result.

"Deal with this?" Sherry said. "A therapist helped me. I didn't learn until my daughter was twenty-six years old that it wasn't my fault, that when the baby separates from the placenta, that happens. It's something I feel almost every day. But I rarely talk about it. I guess I'm afraid of being judged.

"I can't change it. It will always be there. I don't visit her often. She doesn't know me. She doesn't know anyone. Sometimes I get afraid, afraid I'll cry and never stop. I just feel a tiny bit at a time. Tiny bit. Like sticking my toe in hot water. It's still real hot and hurts but where my toe is right now I can deal with.

"That's why I do things like martial arts and fishing," Sherry said. "Those things get me out of my head and into my life. They really do help. Everything I've been through has made me really strong. But there's a thin line between strong and callused."

Many people (including me) have ongoing battles with guilt over the choices we've made.

Most of us find some relief by making amends the best that we can for the things we've done wrong and the choices we've made that have caused others pain. Then we try to deal with that ongoing sense that everything we do is wrong by talking and reasoning things out and trying to stay out of our heads and living our lives the best we can each day.

This is what I've learned: if I can't completely forgive myself, redeeming my mistakes by using them to help others is the next best thing.

"We will not regret the past nor wish to shut the door on it. We will comprehend the word *serenity* and we will know peace. No matter how far down the scale we have gone, we will see how our experience can benefit others." That's what the *Big Book of Alcoholics Anonymous* promises if we do a few simple things.

I was wrong about my interpretation of what the yoga instructor said.

———

Compassion isn't something we think. It's something we do. And it's our choice, too.

Okay. Get ready. We're going to Tibet.

STAYING ON TRACK

"There's a rhythm and an order to life," a friend said. "We don't always like it. But the order doesn't much care whether we like it or not."

Joe and I got off the plane in Lhasa and looked around. Behind the crowd, Lami stood waving at us. We had gone to Tibet at the tail end of the China trip, staying only long enough to make Lami's acquaintance, realize how high the altitude was and how tired we were, and then go home.

Now, six months later, I was back, rested and ready for mountain number five—the grandest holy mountain of them all—Mount Kailash.

The legend is that circling the mountain once clears karma from one life. I believe in the forgiveness of sins. But that's different from karma. It's different from clearing the negative energy from things that we've done. And it's different from forgiving ourselves.

Something had been drawing me to Kailash, inexplicably pulling me toward it, since I first thought about visiting Tibet.

Mount Kailash was the real reason I had trudged through China, walking up all those steps. I wanted to get here, but I needed to go there first. I didn't know what it had to teach me, but for a long time, Kailash had been calling my name. It was the culmination of this spiritual quest.

Joe and I spent a week in Lhasa acclimating to the high altitude there. I was dizzy, breathless, off balance—hypoxic—for days. Toward the end of the week, I could climb stairs. Then I did a *kora*—a circular trek—around the city celebrating the Festival of Enlightenment, with Lami, Joe, and the pilgrims who had traveled to Tibet. Because I was able to do the *kora*, Lami figured I was ready for higher altitudes.

We set out for Kailash in a Jeep, followed by a truck filled with camping and cooking supplies. With altitudes ranging from sixteen thousand to twenty-two thousand feet, Kailash was going to be the highest place we had traveled yet. Each town and village along the way to Kailash would be at an increasingly high altitude.

Lami took us slowly at first, spending only four or five hours a day traveling, so our bodies could adjust to the increasingly thin air. The higher the altitude, the less oxygen you get with each breath. The diminishing return of oxygen at higher altitudes works similar to the Richter scale with earthquakes—as the numbers go up, it doesn't increase an increment with each step. Each increased level of altitude was doubly or triply more severe than the last because of the body's severe response to less and less air.

On the fourth day, we stopped for lunch at a guest house in a small village along the way. It was one of those places that felt like home the moment I walked in. Amada, the woman who owned it, chattered and smiled as she cooked lunch. She showed me pictures of her family and asked about mine. Lami translated, but nobody needs to translate a smile.

I wouldn't mind staying here, I thought as we loaded into the

Jeep. There was no electricity in this village. But it was clean and filled with love. We headed down a bumpy dirt road—more like a path—to our destination of the day: a river seven hours away.

I felt increasingly irritable as we drove mile after mile. Bathroom breaks were annoyingly difficult. All the men had to do was stand outside the Jeep and face the opposite direction from me. For me, a bathroom break meant walking across stretches of terrain until I could hide behind a rock. I found myself stumbling, almost too tired to walk. By the time we arrived at the river, I just wanted to go to bed.

"You have to eat, Meldid," Lami said. "You must keep up your strength."

I sat in the dinner tent eating finger chips and *tsampa*—a Tibetan barley similar to oatmeal. Suddenly, I burst into tears.

Joe looked up from his dinner. "Is something actually the matter?" he said. "Or are you just acting like a chick?"

I apologized, said I didn't know what was wrong, then quickly dried my eyes before Lami came back into the tent. I didn't want him to see me crying. I needed to get a grip. We were on a quest.

We were mountain climbers now.

I finished eating dinner and crawled into my tent. About midnight I startled awake. I was gasping. Choking. Panicked. Struggling for each breath.

Joe woke up and looked at me.

"What's wrong?" he said.

"The air is too thin," I said. "I can't breathe."

The irritability. The crying jag at dinner. The stumbling around. We had ascended too fast. My body wasn't adjusting. Why hadn't I seen this coming on?

Joe looked at me. His eyes reflected my fear.

I had read all about altitude sickness in the travel guides. I knew it could come on quickly. I knew it could be fatal, and fatal fast. The only cure was to get to a lower altitude so the body could get enough air.

I dug in my backpack and pulled out a can of oxygen. I didn't have much left. I spaced out the oxygen, made it last as long as I could. When the can was empty, I lay down. *Be cool*, I thought. *Just relax and breathe.*

It didn't work. No matter how hard I tried not to, I was gasping for air and panicking when I couldn't get enough. Joe left the tent. He returned moments later with two more cans of oxygen.

"This is all there is in the truck," he said. "Try to make it last through the night. We can't travel until daylight. It'd be too hard to cross the river and too dangerous to maneuver the roads."

At the first hint of dawn, Lami and Joe loaded me into the back of the Jeep.

I collapsed—stretched out—on the backseat listening to Lami and Joe talk as we bumped our way back across seven hours of rocky Tibetan roads.

"Two men have died on the mountain this past month from altitude sickness. Our trip to Kailash is canceled," Lami said. "It's too dangerous to go back. If we can get Meldid well, you will either have to think of something else you want to do in Tibet—or just go home."

This was one of those rare occasions where I was too weak and beaten to try to control. I couldn't argue. I just wanted air.

As we descended to lower altitudes, I gradually found myself able to sit up. Five hundred meters can make a tremendous difference for someone who's altitude sick. As soon as I could breathe a little more comfortably, I started thinking about something besides air.

Let this whole trip go down the drain? Are they nuts? No, no, I thought. *It was the reason—the purpose—behind climbing all those other mountains first. I was doing that just to get here. Now they're telling me I can't go?* I thought about the other options in Tibet: Mount Everest, Lhasa. *Nope, won't do. Kailash is the only place I want to go.*

I sat up and leaned over the front seat.

"How about this, Lami? Instead of heading back toward Shigatse, let's go back to Amada's guest house. We can stay there for a day or so. See if I can get well. Then we'll meditate. Pray. I've got a plan. If it works—if it feels right—maybe we can try to slowly go back?"

Lami scowled at me.

"You don't have to answer," I said. "Just think about it for a while."

I wasn't willing to give up. Not yet.

I had been so certain I could just go to Kailash. I hadn't prayed. I hadn't meditated. I had assumed. On this trip, each time we had gone over a high mountain pass, Lami and the driver had raised their hands and chanted, "*Soe, soe, soe, soe, soe, soe, soe.*" It was a way of asking for blessing and permission to safely pass over this high place, a way of showing respect to the powers that be in their world.

"We have an old story in Tibet," Lami had said at dinner one night. "Say that a man needs money badly. He goes out to his car and looks down at the ground. He sees a hundred-dollar bill. He looks around. There is no one in sight—no one that the money could possibly belong to. He bends down and picks up the money. He can do one of two things. He can say, *Look how clever and powerful I am that I found this money.* Or he can look to the heavens and say, *Thank you—what a blessed man I am.*

I couldn't control this trip.

But *maybe* I could get a blessing from God.

"So Buddhists, Christians, and even recovery programs all talk about the same thing," a friend said one day. "They all say that desire is the root of all people's suffering. So does that mean that we should just walk around not wanting anything?"

I thought about the question. Seemed like a Zen riddle to me. I wanted to come up with the right answer, but I didn't know what that answer was. Do we take the risk of wanting anything? Isn't that self-will? But then is self-will wrong? And if it's wrong, why were we given that gift?

My friend didn't wait for me to answer. He answered instead.

"The answer is no. If we walk around not wanting anything, that means we've most likely gone numb."

There's a way of being alive where we don't take any risks. We don't want anything. We don't try anything. We've protected ourselves so much we're numb. We don't have to work that hard at letting go of anything because we haven't allowed ourselves to want anything that much. We say, *whatever,* not from a place of compassion and letting go but from a place of resigned callousness.

We think that keeps us safe and gives us a little control.

There's another way to be in the world where we're alive and awake. We're filled with passion, dreams, hopes, and desires.

The prayer I said was simple. It's short and a popular one. I looked up at the heavens and said, "Thy will be done."

In this section we'll look at some stories about people who glimpsed a deeper meaning and order in life. So what do we do now that we're awake and on fire with hopes, dreams, plans, ambitions, passion, needs, fears, doubts, and desires? The secret is constantly surrendering our free will to God.

Don't just *trudge* the road of happy destiny—although sometimes that's the best we can do. Tap into the rhythm of life.

Learn to dance.

1

They Dug Deeper

—————

Marge Rieder, Ph.D., a hypnotherapist in Lake Elsinore, California—the small town where I skydive—began to put a puzzle together one ordinary day in 1986. She was working with a client, Maureen Williamson, hypnotizing her to help her deal with some issues that were bothering her.

Rieder's practice of twenty years at the time was devoted to helping people do things like quit smoking, understand their phobias and fears, and find things they had lost by digging into the power of their subconscious minds. Williamson came to Rieder that day with a piece of paper on which she had written a name. The name was John Daniel Ashford. Williamson had written it down one day when she was in a restaurant eating a piece of carrot cake. Williamson didn't know anyone by this name. She wanted to find out what the name meant, and why she had remembered it.

Under hypnotism, a story of another time and place began to emerge. The time was during the Civil War. The place was Millboro, Virginia. Over the following months, as Williamson was hypnotized, it came out that thirty-five people who lived in the Lake Elsinore area were identified as having lived in Millboro during the Civil War. Most of their lives were intertwined then, as they were today.

Rieder broadened her sessions to include some of these thirty-five people. During hypnotherapy, the people revealed details of houses, buildings, waterfalls, and tunnels from the small Virginia town. They also recalled the stories of their lives back then—stories of war, tragedy, murder, intrigue, betrayal, love, friendship, and day-to-day life.

On an expedition to Millboro, Rieder and two clients confirmed almost all of the details that had emerged in hypnotherapy—houses, buildings, locations of tunnels used to store war supplies and hide slaves, and little-known nicknames and stories about these events.

Even Rieder herself, it turned out, had been involved in the lives of these people and the story from that time. Neither Rieder nor her clients had been to Millboro before. Except for two people, they hadn't heard of this place until the name came up under hypnosis.

Yet they were able to recall in detail the town, the people they had lived with, and the emotions involved with that life. Rieder wrote a book, *Mission to Millboro,* in 1993. The book received national acclaim.

What does Rieder make of the picture that the pieces of the puzzle created?

"Never, at any time, was it my intention to 'prove the theory of reincarnation,' per se," she wrote. "Not entirely discounting reincarnation, I tend to lean heavily toward Carl Jung's theories of the collective unconscious and archetypes. . . .

"Call it archetypal memory or reincarnation—these words are only labels. There is little room for doubt that we all have memories of past lifetimes deep in our minds and that it is the combination of these memories that constitutes the basis for our psyche today."

• • •

Some events in life can't be rationally explained.

Some people believe in reincarnation. Some don't.

Some religions subscribe to those beliefs.

As a journalist, I'm not certain. My jury is out.

What most religions and therapists agree upon is that the purpose or message of reincarnation—for those who believe—isn't to remember being a princess or a king in some other far-off distant time. It's not to perpetuate the victim-perpetrator belief—*Oh, I'm doing this to you because you did this to me another time.*

The purpose that is most valid, therapists and religions agree, is to explain that there may be a larger picture to the game of cause and effect. And, as Rieder said, a deeper realm to the human mind.

The subjects of the subconscious mind, past lives, reincarnation, and life after death have been in the forefront of our culture for many years. What do you believe?

Is it hogwash, hooey, or fact?

I was talking to a friend one day. She had been through a lot of hard lessons. We were talking about why, what to make of this thing called life. I brought up the subject of reincarnation. Told her I didn't know for sure. "It's kind of like insurance, though," I said. "Even the remotest possibility that it may be true—that I may have to come back and repeat all these experiences again if I don't learn what I came to learn—is enough to make me stick around this time and try my best to get it right."

————

"What does 'getting it right' mean?" she asked after a while.

"I'm not entirely certain about that, either," I said.

"But I think what it means is opening our hearts."

A Curious Table

A single parent, Don had recently moved to a small town in the middle of nowhere after finishing raising his daughter and finding himself in an empty nest. He had met some new people there. Things evolved. He was a contractor. One of the people he met was remodeling a house; he ended up making friends and moving in. A series of coincidences and choices evolved.

Don was surprised when his roommate brought home the small, curious-looking yellow end table. "Where'd you get that?" he asked.

"I found it at the antique store," he explained. "I thought it would be a good table to put over there—for the telephone."

Don began pointing to each mark and stain on the old table, obviously an odd one and most likely one of a kind. "That came when I stored a can of oil on it in the garage," he said.

Then he carefully explained each of the other idiosyncrasies about the table. It had belonged to him over thirty years ago. He and his family had given it away when they moved from the area to another part of the United States.

"Don't you think that's odd?" he asked. "Don't you think it's curious that table would come full circle like that—and end up back with me?"

Many of us find meaning in the little things in life—whether we call them signs, markers, or guidance—that reassure us that there's some kind of order, we may be on track, and there is some kind of Divine Plan.

It's easy to wonder as we make our choices the best we can—combined with circumstance, fate, and the things we can't chose—if we're on our path. Am I where I'm meant to be? Have I wandered off? Is there a reason I'm here? Should I be someplace else?

When things start going wrong and collapsing around us—particularly in the areas of finance, health, and romance—we wonder if we're doing something *wrong*. While most people agree that it's important to look for the lesson if and when things start falling apart, it's not necessarily a sign that we're on the wrong path.

Life may be trying to get our attention, point something out. It may be a natural cycle in our lives—a cycle that we didn't know about or expect. Or it may be something else.

When I hit a wall—when I can't move forward—it's usually a sign there's a lesson at hand, something I'm not seeing either because I'm trying to control everything or because I'm moving too fast. I usually have a process I go through—stubbornness, trying to control things, trying to push through that wall, and thinking that everything is a mistake. I usually go through this process first, before I'm ready to become willing to learn.

"I'm walking through that swamp again, wearing those concrete boots," I said to a friend.

"Well, all that probably means is that life is trying to slow you down so you don't miss something that it wants you to see," she said.

How do you determine if you're on track or not? Many of us have silly little signs that other people think are weird, but those signs can mean a lot to us. Trusting ourselves—based on listening to what others say and our own inner voice—is a choice.

Believing that there's a Plan is usually a good bet, too. The path is rarely smooth. Sometimes the lessons we learn repeat themselves. Surrendering control and asking, *What am I learning now?* isn't something we do just once.

Most of us find ourselves making that hard call at least once a day.

Sometimes a wall isn't really a wall. It's just the next obstacle on the course.

When in doubt, don't assume. Ask.

She Made a Good Call

Corinne Edwards looked at her watch, then shrugged her shoulders and began interviewing her first guest. His name was Larry Dossey. He was a doctor who had written about the power of combining medicine with prayer—and the power of thought as a form of prayer.

Corinne is a good TV host. She takes her guests and their work seriously. She reads their books, and she is genuinely interested in each subject she discusses. Her cameraman signaled a break.

"Your next guest isn't here yet, Corinne," he said.

"No problem," Corinne said. She knew something her cameraman didn't. She knew her next guest would show.

I was scheduled to do a closing speech at a fund-raiser in Minnesota. It was part of a mini-tour I had agreed to do some time ago. It was nearing time for me to get onstage. It was a fund-raiser to raise money to send adolescents to chemical-dependency treatment, an issue I deeply believed in during a time when people were wondering if that was a good place for extra money in our world to go.

At the fund-raiser, as the time for me to speak neared, my stomach starting hurting. Aching badly. I could hardly sit up. I felt sweaty, nauseous, cramped, sick. I excused myself from the table, went to the rest room, and splashed cold water on my face. I needed to pull it together, do what I came here to do.

Luckily it was the end of the evening and my bit was small. I had gone through the drill of public speaking enough to do what I needed to do, even sick. *Thank God for podiums,* I thought, giving my little spiel. *If I didn't have something to hold myself up with, I'd fall down.*

I got back to my hotel room about eleven o'clock that night. I didn't know if I had caught a virus or if I'd eaten some bad food, but I was sick. Really ill. I ordered some tea and water from room service and tried to calm my stomach. I was supposed to get up at 4 A.M. and fly down to Chicago to make an appearance on a TV show. That left me five hours to get feeling better and get at least a fair night's sleep. At one o'clock I was still awake, lying in bed in the fetal position with a bad stomachache.

The most sleep I can possibly get now is three hours, I thought, staring at the clock like it was my enemy. *It's not looking good for tomorrow's television show.*

At quarter to two I got up and called my publicist's cell phone. "Call Corinne Edwards. Give her my apologies," I said. "I'm really sick. I just can't go."

I'd never be able to fly down to Chicago feeling this way, with two hours of sleep. I canceled my wakeup call, too. Once I fell asleep, I wanted to sleep for as long as I could and give my body a chance to rest and heal. Somewhere between two and two-thirty I finally dozed off.

When I woke up I looked at the clock, wondering how long I'd slept.

It was only four in the morning! What was I doing up now? I closed my eyes, rolled over, and tried to get back to sleep. I couldn't. I groaned, pulled the covers over my head. By now I was squeezing my eyes shut. *Arrrrgh! Okay. Alright already*, I thought. I dragged my tired weak body out of bed. *I can't do this. I'm not doing this. I've already canceled,* I thought. At the same time I was thinking that, I was throwing on some clothes and grabbing my purse.

Whoever I was arguing with was winning, because I walked out the door, despite my complaints, drove to the airport, and got on that plane.

I walked into the TV studio looking like something the proverbial cat dragged in. The makeup lady did her magic. *Thank God for face paint*, I thought, looking in the mirror. I was looking and feeling almost human by the time I went onstage.

I did the interview with Corinne. She wanted to talk about *Codependent No More*. It was the fifteenth anniversary of that book. I liked her interview. She had read the book. Seemed interested in it and in me. More than that, she seemed to genuinely care about the viewers watching her show.

When the interview ended, she invited me to stay for pizza and Coke. I thanked her, but declined. "I'm still weak and sick. I didn't sleep last night. In fact, I wasn't planning on coming here today," I said. Then I explained what had happened to me. "I'm surprised I showed," I said.

"I'm not," she said back.

We talked about some things we had in common. She shared with me that she was a widow, and had written a book, *Reflections from a Woman Alone*. "Did you know that I have a son who died, too?"

I said I didn't know that, and told her I was sorry about her loss.

"I've been trying to get you on my show for five years," Corinne said. "Whenever I'd call your publicist, they'd just tell me that

Melody doesn't go on the road anymore. Finally they called me and told me you were doing some media this fall. I was so excited. Yesterday I had the funniest feeling, like something was wrong. So I just asked God and my son—the one that passed over—to make sure to get you here no matter what."

Each of us has a different explanation for the events that transpire in our lives. It may not make sense to others. I'm not sure that it matters as long as it makes sense to us. There's more to life than we can see with our eyes. Remember, the sun isn't rising or setting—it's standing still.

Some things are true whether we see—and believe—them or not.

It's God's will.

People said that to me when my son died. They said it to me when my marriage went bad, and I lost all those dreams and hopes. Usually it's something that people say when things turn sour and we're in a lot of pain.

It may be true, but it's not a comforting thing to hear. Usually when I need to be held in God's arms the most, someone is screaming at me that God wants me to feel the way that I don't want to feel and wants me to lose whatever I've just lost.

I think what people are really trying to say is: there's a Plan. It may not feel good right now, but if you go through this pain, things are going to work out. In my younger days, I could look at a situation and see only one or two possibilities for how things could work out. The older I've gotten, the more I've seen that there are ways things can work out that I could spend a lifetime trying to imagine and not even come close.

Sometimes walking our path and living our lives is like putting a big jigsaw puzzle together. The problem usually is that we don't know what the whole picture looks like and we often don't have all the pieces yet. We get them—sometimes one by one—as we go through the days.

I was talking to a woman one day after she had just finished going through an excruciatingly painful six months. Things had not gone the way she hoped and planned. She wondered a lot of the time why so many things were going wrong. Then in one moment—as can happen sometimes—the final piece of the puzzle came into place. She saw how everything worked out, and how everything worked out well—better than it would have had she done it herself.

———

"Don't you just love God's will?" she said.
"Yes, I do," I said. "But not usually while
it's working itself out."

GOING TOWARD THE LIGHT

"So how do you know if you're making the right choice?" a woman asked me one day. "And what if you don't make the right one?"

"If we're on our path, we'll know," I said. "And even the wrong choices will eventually take us back to where we belong."

"Oh, I get it," she said. "All roads lead home."

It felt like coming home when we pulled into the village where Amada ran her guest house. I tried to hide the stagger in my walk as I made my way up to the patio and eating area overlooking the parking lot. I didn't want to worry Lami. I was feeling better, but I was still weak. I knew I had been very sick.

It was a quiet moment. I doubt that anyone who looked at me knew what I was doing. It looked like I was just sitting there, staring into space. I was actually praying and doing my best to surrender to God.

There is a peace that comes when we say *Thy will be done* and mean it. But I also made it clear to God what I would like—to go to the mountain and complete this trip.

I had met and talked with a woman when we were at Amada's earlier, when we stopped for lunch. The woman was from San Francisco; she and her group had stopped there to eat on their way back from Kailash on their way to Nepal. I had asked her if she had a problem with the altitude.

"Not a bit," she said. "I took Diamox."

If I could get my hands on some Diamox—a Western medication for altitude sickness—and my body reacted positively to the medication, maybe I could complete this trip. If not, I'd give up, do some sightseeing, write it off to experience, and just go home.

I sat on the patio for a while. Then I went inside to talk to Amada.

"I would like to buy some clothing from you," I said. (Her daughter translated for us.) "I have been wearing hiking clothes for almost a week. It doesn't work well for women in this part of the world."

There were few rest room facilities around. Long skirts were a practical matter in Tibet. It was an easy way for women to create a rest room anywhere they went—a matter of survival here. I was weary from walking and walking, looking for privacy everywhere I went.

Amada smiled, then opened a big dresser drawer on the back wall in the dining room. Within minutes, I was wearing a shimmering pink blouse and a long dress.

Sometimes doing the little things that make us more comfortable and relieve stress can make a big difference in how we feel.

I went back to the patio and waited to see what would take place next.

Within an hour, a tour bus heading from Mount Kailash back to Nepal stopped at Amada's. I pulled the driver aside. "I need some help," I said.

I had read about Diamox in the travel guide before the woman from San Francisco had told me about it. Some people who took Diamox had no problems with the medicine, or with high altitudes once the medicine was in their bloodstream. Others had adverse effects: the medication didn't help with the altitude; instead, the medicine made them sick. I didn't like the idea of taking medicine without a doctor's prescription, but I knew that some of the tour guides carried it in case of emergency.

This was an emergency, as far as I was concerned.

After bartering with the tour guide for a while, I purchased enough Diamox to get me through the journey to Kailash—and a case of oxygen.

If the medication worked, all I had to do was convince Lami that it was okay for us to slowly make our way back. I took a small amount, my first dose. It seemed to help.

I told Lami I was feeling better, and that if the medicine continued to work, I wanted to try traveling to Kailash again. "We can spend the night here tonight and I'll rest. Then we can leave in the morning. We can take it slowly," I said. "The altitude at the river will be our test. If I can make it through the night there, we'll proceed. If not, we'll come back. I'll concede."

Lami agreed.

"Meldid, I believe the mountain wants you to visit it," he said. "Going back also feels right to me."

That night, before we went to sleep, Amada and Lami entered my room in the guest house. A yak-dung fire was burning in the potbelly stove. Incense gently perfumed the room. I felt as at home and comfortable as I did anywhere in the world. It still surprises me how all you need to make a home is a feeling of safety and love.

They sat down, said they had something to ask.

"Sure," I said. "Ask away."

"A monk has made his way here from eastern Tibet. It has taken him over a year to get here. He has been hiding out here for months, waiting for the right person to come along. It is his life's dream to make the pilgrimage all the way to Kailash," Lami said. "It is very dangerous for him to travel; the Chinese government would arrest him and put him in jail. Would you be willing to hide him in the back of your truck and take him as far as you could?"

I said yes.

People say everything happens for a reason and things work out for good. But I still like it when I get to see a piece or a bit of what that reason is.

The next day we headed back to the river, the monk tucked safely away. Before we reached the border check, we stopped and let him out of the truck. If he scurried behind the mountains and walked fast, he could pass the checkpoint, make it to the next village, catch another ride there, and be at Kailash by the end of the week.

We made camp at the river that evening. I was skittish about going to sleep, remembering how ill and panicked I had become the last time I was here. I tried to stay calm. I lay down. Closed my eyes. When I woke up, it was morning.

I felt fine.

Well, not *fine*. I still wasn't up to par. But at least I could breathe.

We made a decision to proceed to Kailash. It was a calculated risk. We were all aware of that. If I got sick now, help would be two days away. But I appeared to be holding my own.

That evening as we neared the mountain, Lami turned to me with a serious look on his face.

"Meldid, you've made it this far. I'm sorry to say this and it causes me pain, but I cannot allow you to walk around the mountain. It is a hard trail. Many people die making that pilgrimage. It would be dangerous for all of us if anything happened to you."

I felt instantly sad. I knew Lami was right. *But at least I could go to the mountain*, I thought. *That's mostly my dream.* We drove for another hour or so. When we approached the mountain, the car stalled. Lami and the driver got out to tinker with the carburetor. Joe turned to me.

"I have something to tell you, too," he said. "And I feel awkward saying it. I can't tell you exactly why this happened. But for the past hour I've been feeling it so strongly I know it's true. You know I'm not a particularly spiritual guy. I'm a mountain climber, a camper." He held out his wrist bearing his expensive, trendy watch. "And I'm a yuppie, too."

Joe stopped talking and just stared at me. He was at a loss for words.

"So what's the point?" I finally said.

"I know in my heart that the reason we made this trip together is because I'm supposed to make the pilgrimage around Kailash for you. I don't know about all this karma jazz. And I don't have any beliefs one way or another about past lives. Maybe the past-life thing is real; maybe not. Maybe I owe you this for something I did to you in another life. Or maybe karma works another way. Maybe it's like a big universal bank. And it doesn't really matter who owes what to whom: if you've got it coming, you're going to be paid. And the universe will put the person in your life they can use to pay you with.

"So when we get to that mountain, I want you to focus on the mountain, your life, and the blessings you want to receive while I walk around it. And any merit that can be obtained from the pilgrimage, I dedicate to you."

Well, I started crying. For a second I thought Joe did, too. But it was hard to tell. He was that kind of a guy.

I started to protest, but Joe stood firm.

This wasn't exactly what I had planned, but it felt really good.

It took Joe two days of walking, but he made it around that mountain—trendy hiking boots, camping gear, and all.

The two men driving the trucks decided to circumnavigate the mountain, too, as long as we were there. Lami urged them to do it. Said it would be good for their souls. They scurried around it in one day.

When they returned, they were smiling. They pointed to their feet. We looked down. They had worn bedroom slippers around that treacherous trail. They had holes in the bottom of their slippers.

"It was good," they said. "But now we need new shoes."

The lesson from Kailash was clear. It's been said by many experts, teachers, and religions. *Everything will be okay in the end. And if things aren't okay, it's not over yet.*

"What's the most important thing I can do for my spiritual growth once I return home?" I asked Lami on the way back to Lhasa.

"Meldid, if someone can just spend five or ten minutes a day praying and meditating, it will change that person's life," he said. "And when you pray, don't just say fearfully *please give me this or that*, thinking *I'll never get it anyway*. It's important that at least a little bit, you believe you'll receive what you ask."

I chuckled at Lami's answer. Here I was, expecting all this magic, mystery, and wisdom from Tibet. And he told me something that Twelve-Step programs had been telling people for a long time: meditate and pray a little each day.

Remember the Butterfly Effect? One choice with enough butterflies flapping their wings thrown in can be the gateway to heaven or hell? In this section we'll look at some stories about how we can throw in a few butterflies of our own. The secret is believing that everything—every single thing in our lives—happens for a reason. There are no wasted events. But there's more to life than meets the eye. That means we don't always get to *see* what that reason is.

Maybe the Golden Rule still does work, after all.

He Ran Out of Hope

He sat in his kitchen surrounded by hidden bottles of gin. Like most alcoholics, he drank for no other reason than *it was there*. *Sinking in quicksand* is the phrase he used to describe himself and his life. He couldn't stop on his own.

A friend came to visit that day.

He told him about a way to stop. The program of action his friend suggested was simple but not easy. He needed to search his soul and his life and make amends for the wrongs he had done. He needed to give up his self-serving ways and think about others instead of just himself. He needed to humbly ask God for guidance, then when in doubt sit quietly and wait for the answer to come.

He needed to reacquaint himself with God.

Bill Wilson could understand the importance of getting right with others and himself. But God? He believed in God generally, but as he looked around at the world—the wars and treachery going on—he surmised that evil ruled both the world and his own life. The idea of a personal God was foreign to him.

Bill's friend then suggested that Bill chose his own conception of God.

That day changed Bill's life and the world. It was the day that sparked the movement called Alcoholics Anonymous. Bill Wilson thought that thousands of lives might be impacted by this way of life. He was wrong. Alcoholics Anonymous has saved millions of people who lost all hope. Even Bill's tragic story before that day— all the events that led to it—were put to good use.

An important part of the actions Bill took was reacquainting himself with God through *prayer*. It helped catapult him into that spiritual realm he called *the fourth dimension of existence*. He learned that A Power Greater Than Himself could do for him what he could not do for himself.

You don't have to be a hopeless alcoholic to benefit from prayer. Prayer doesn't change *things*. Prayer changes *us*.

Did you ever call someone on the phone, planning on leaving a message on the voice mail because you expected them not to be home or not to answer the phone? That's how it was for me the first time I sincerely talked to God.

I had been exposed to God and prayer when I was a child. I attended church from an early age. I went to a religious academy for most of my high school years. But at age twelve, I decided that if God was real, He didn't care about me. And as dastardly as the events in my life had been until that time, I decided I could handle things at least as well on my own.

When I ended up in treatment for my chemical dependency in 1973, I was horrified to discover something that people around me had known for a while—I couldn't stop using on my own. I was facing a jail sentence or indefinite treatment. *Treatment for as long as it takes* were the words the District Court Judge used who had sentenced me there.

I had already been there a long time—months—and I was still

getting high in treatment the day I decided to talk to God again. "God, I don't know if you're real or not. And I don't know if there's a program that can help me get better or not. But if you are real, and if there is, please help me get it," I said.

That's all. A simple prayer.

I looked at the ceiling, doubting it had been heard.

I was astounded when within a few days I was sitting on the banks of the hospital grounds—getting high—and had a psychic transformation that revolutionized my life. I took a hit off a joint and lay back on the lawn, expecting to watch the clouds roll by. Instead, the heavens took on a purplish tone. And I knew that I knew that I knew that moment that I had no right to keep getting high.

I took one more hit off the joint, then went back into the hospital and began to throw myself into the program with all the commitment I had previously dedicated to getting high.

If I take just half the energy I've put into screwing up and use it trying to do the right thing, there's little in this world I can't do, I thought.

I didn't tell anyone about that experience for years. *I'm already indefinitely committed to an institution. If I tell people the heavens turned purple and I saw God, I'll never get out,* I thought.

I didn't expect God to answer when I called Him on the phone.

It wasn't that God became real that day. He became real to me.

"I was fishing one day. It was a stupid thing," a woman told me. "But it meant a lot to me. I stuck my line in the water and asked God, if He was real, to help me catch a fish. And I did. I caught the biggest fish I've ever snagged in my life. It wasn't about catching that fish, though," she said. "It was about establishing a personal relationship with God."

We can talk to God formally—using the prayers recommended by our religion. We can pray in the morning, in the evening, or throughout the day. Some people even ascribe to the belief that our thoughts and intentions are like prayers.

We can keep a prayer journal—either a diary, or a file in our computer. This is an idea that's particularly helpful to me. I like the written word. It has power. When I write something, it becomes more real. I can also look back at my prayers and see how they've been answered. Keeping a journal of answered prayers helps me remember to have faith during those valley experiences, too.

We can talk to God informally throughout the day, shooting thoughts to our conception of God as we understand God. We can pray out loud or silently.

The components of prayer that are common to most if not all religions include confession of wrongdoing, asking for forgiveness and cleansing for wrongdoing, acknowledgment of blessings and answers to prayer that have been received, praise (or general thankfulness), requests for guidance to stay on the path, requests for help with specific problems, and blessings on the people in our lives.

I like to talk to God generally, too—just ramble on about what I'm feeling, what I'm thinking, where I'm at.

Sometimes the most powerful prayer we can pray is simply *Thy will be done.*

"Your relationship with God has been as passionate as your relationship with any human being," a friend remarked to me one day. That's probably true. I've been delighted with, infuriated with, complacent toward, dutiful toward, resentful of, humbled before, and eternally grateful to God at any given point in my life. And sometimes all of the above in the same day.

By the way, while we're asking blessings for everyone else, why not take a minute and ask God to bless us, too?

———

Prayer is a choice.
Don't be surprised when God answers the phone.

2

She Couldn't Sit Still

———

Lisa sat on the cushion on the floor, squinting her eyes shut. She wiggled. She squirmed. Her back ached. She wondered when she was going to meet her soul mate. She worried about having enough money to pay her bills. She peeked out of her eyes.

The happy little nun was supposed to teach Lisa how to meditate.

The nun was meditating just fine. She looked like she was in a trance.

Lisa closed her eyes again. She tried to erase all thoughts from her mind, but the thoughts kept pouring in.

"Okay," Lisa finally said when she couldn't sit any longer. "I'm done. How long has it been?"

The nun opened her eyes.

"Seven minutes," she said.

A Psalm from the Old Testament says, "Be Still and Know that I am God." Many of us have no problem knowing that God is God. The hard part is being still.

Read a daily meditation book. Go to yoga class. Relax in a hot tub. Take a walk. Two ideas are involved with developing a personal relationship with anyone: talking, and listening.

You can't hear unless you're being quiet.

Shhhhh.

Be still. Focus on something other than what you're able to think about on your own—a virtue, a higher ideal, a place or an idea that brings peace.

Or leave an empty quiet space. Ask God to fill that up.

If you can't sit still for seven minutes, then do less.

———

Meditating for five minutes a day can change your life.

3

He Saw the Future

Michael Bodine had *the gift* since he was a child. He could see and hear things that others couldn't. He could communicate with *the other side*. A woman came to him. She didn't consider herself that type. She was a Christian and skeptical of psychics. But she couldn't take her life any longer. She wanted some answers. And she wanted them now.

Her questions were typical of most people who came to see him. They wanted to know about love, money, children, career, health, and sex.

"When is my life going to change?" she asked.

He listened quietly to the things only he could hear.

"Opportunities for change are all around you," he said. "And they have been for quite some time. But nothing outside of you is going to change until you make a choice."

"How will I know which opportunities are right for me? Which ones I should pursue?" she asked.

He pointed out some opportunities that she had missed. He gave her some specifics about opportunities that he saw coming to pass.

"Most people come to see me because they're waiting for something or someone outside of themselves to change," he said. "And sometimes the problem—the issue—is a timing thing. But the last thing in the world that people want to hear is that if they want change to happen, they've got to do something differently themselves.

"When I look at people's lives I see opportunities all around them, every day. The hard part about seeing so much about people is that I see how many opportunities people let slip by. Life isn't holding them back. They're holding themselves back by not listening to their intuition and then making a choice."

Some people call it a gut reaction. Others, intuition, or a sixth sense. There are two kinds of feelings in life: the emotional ones, and how a thing feels to us.

I felt scared, hopeless, and depressed when I couldn't find work. But it was my intuition, that sixth sense, that guided me about where to look.

I was grief-stricken, crushed, nearly destroyed when my son, Shane, died. I couldn't think of what to do next, because my grief had wiped out my rational mind. It was a quieter voice that guided me about how to get through the moments of each day.

Both kinds of feelings matter. The emotional ones need to be felt and released so we can hear those quieter ones, because they're the ones that guide us along our path.

Self-care isn't a static science.

It's a constantly evolving art.

————

If there's one rule for taking care of ourselves, it's this:
struggle through things until you learn to trust yourself.

4

She Learned Nonattachment

———

She watched her husband drinking himself to death, destroying her family, her finances, their love.

"You can't do anything about him," her best friend said. "But you can change yourself."

When Elaine was first introduced to the concept of letting go—nonattachment—she thought it was something she was going to need to do only once or twice in her life. It was a difficult concept to grasp—how to love people, how to care, how to be intimately involved with life without clinging and holding on to people, places, and things.

"At first I thought my husband was just a jerk and I needed to let go of only him. Twenty years have passed. The lesson has been ground into me. I've had to let go of him. My children grew up and left home. They had issues along the way. I've had to let go of them, too.

"Slowly the message sank in. Letting go wasn't something I needed to do just once or twice. My alcoholic husband was the vehicle to introducing me to nonattachment as a way of life."

• • •

"You can't make him stop drinking, Melody, but you can go to Al-Anon."

"You can't do anything about that—whatever that problem you can't solve is—but you can go see a movie. Do something—anything—that feels good to you."

Sometimes I get like a dog with a bone. All I can see and focus on is the one thing I can't do anything about, and I chew on it and gnash my teeth until I wear myself out. Part of letting go means switching our focus from trying to do the impossible to doing something we can do. It might not solve the problem, but it helps us relax and feel better while we wait and see how things work out.

Sometimes the little things we do in life mean a lot.

"The last years of my father's life, I used to visit him and feel so bad that he was living alone," a woman told me. 'Aren't you lonely?' I'd ask him.

"'Honey, I'm in an intimate relationship with the world,' he'd say."

Nonattachment doesn't mean we don't care.
It isn't something we do only when we're breaking up
with someone. It's a way of life that can enhance all
our relationships. And when we stop clinging so tightly to it—
whether it's a person, place, or thing—we often find we
get a whole lot more back than we released.

5

He Found the Rainbow
and the Pot of Gold

───────

"Here's some money—half of everything I have in this world. Take it, go learn black magic, and don't stop until you get revenge on the people who have done this to us," the woman said to her son. "If you don't do this, I'll kill myself and my death will be on your hands."

Her husband had died; his brother had stolen the inheritance money that belonged to her. Then the brother treated her and her two children cruelly, lower than dirt—like slaves. She was upset. Well, distraught.

It was one thousand years ago in Tibet when the mother spoke those words to Milarepa, her fifteen-year-old son. Many things have changed in our world since then. But the themes of pain, cruelty, loss, disappointment, hatred, revenge, betrayal, and trying to make sense of life haven't.

Whether we throw money at our problems, medicate ourselves, go numb, withdraw, seek revenge, give up, try harder,
manipulate, or learn magic—people still want to gain a sense of
control over their lives. We want what we think will make us
happy. We want what's been taken from or not granted to us,
including our sense of power.

We don't want to feel the pain.

Milarepa, the young man cheated out of his inheritance, did as
his mother asked. He learned black magic (another form of control). Then he successfully cast a spell that killed thirty-five members of his uncle's family and friends. Scorpions or snakes destroyed
a beam at a wedding feast, or so the story goes. The house collapsed,
killing all the guests except for the uncle and his wife, Milarepa's
aunt. Milarepa wanted them to survive so they would know that he
had gotten revenge. He wanted them to feel pain, too.

Just to make sure that his uncle got the message about how
powerful he (Milarepa) had become, he did another spell. He sent a
hailstorm to the village where the uncle lived, destroying all the
crops and instilling more fear. The uncle got the message. The vil-
lagers did, too.

The war was over. Milarepa and his mother had won.

Revenge and victory tasted sweet, as they usually do. Then in
an ugly moment, life twisted again. Milarepa realized what he had
really done. Just as the themes of betrayal, loss, and injustice are
timeless and eternal, another idea was present then that's still
around now. *There's no free lunch. Do unto others as you would have
them do you. Love your neighbor as you love yourself. What comes
around goes around until it lands back in your lap.* And it usually comes
back "bigger and worser than what you sent round in the first
place," wrote J. California Cooper in *The Future Has a Past.*

Milarepa had killed a lot of people. He had caused many others
to lose their livelihoods, loved ones, food, and hope. He was

doomed, his fate stamped, sealed, and about to be delivered. He had sent it to himself. He was a magician. The laws of the land wouldn't get him, but he knew that eventually the Great Law of Cause and Effect—karma—would.

Now it was Milarepa's turn to became distraught and obsessed—not with what had been done to him, but with what he had done to others and consequently to himself. He sought out a teacher, someone to help him turn his life around, repair some of the damage he had done, and get on a better path. Because of Milarepa's despair over the black magic he had done, Milarepa's former teacher decided to end his career in destruction and black magic and seek a better way, too. Eventually Milarepa found a lama, Marpa, who agreed to mentor him. Marpa was considered to be one of the highest lamas of that time. Many believed that the man who instructed Marpa's teacher was a reincarnation of Amitabha— another word for *amitofa*—"Blessing" or "Boundless Light."

In the Western World, we call it *the Grace of God.*

Milarepa decided to turn his life around, but his story didn't end there. He was cheerfully expectant, only to learn that his ordeals had just begun. Marpa the monk agreed to teach Milarepa, but only after Milarepa earned the favor by constructing a tower—a home—for Marpa. Milarepa did as Marpa asked, carrying all the rocks and boulders for construction by hand. Before he finished, though, Marpa told him to tear it down and return all the boulders and stones to their original place. Milarepa complied. Then Marpa told him to build a tower in another place. Before Milarepa could finish this structure, Marpa again changed his mind. This went on for a while. Milarepa wasn't allowed to finish anything he started. He was weak and thin, and, from all the hard labor, his body was covered with sores. He had been repeatedly plunged into abject despair. And Marpa hadn't taught him one thing yet.

Finally Milarepa gave up. He left Marpa and sought enlighten-ment somewhere else. *The reason I can't move forward and this man is jerking me around is probably due to all my karma and all the people I've hurt,* Milarepa thought. *At least I've stopped killing and harming other people. Even if I can't achieve enlightenment this life, maybe I won't have to come back as a scorpion or snake.*

Marpa's wife had encouraged Milarepa to leave Marpa; she helped him raise money and find another teacher. She felt sorry for Milarepa because Marpa was treating him so badly. After a while, Marpa brought Milarepa back to his home. That's when Marpa explained.

"I wasn't torturing you because I'm a jerk," Marpa said. "You had so many negative emotions and so much negative karma from what you had done. You needed those painful experiences to clear the wreckage you caused in your past. You needed to experience that anguish in order to forgive and free yourself. It was part of a spiritual plan.

"You should have been plunged into despair nine times, but it was only eight because my wife, out of pity for you—bless her soul—interfered. But you're clear enough anyway to receive the teachings now. You're ready to stop looking back, go to the next level, and move forward in your life. By the way," Marpa added, "it's possible to achieve enlightenment in just one life. Yes, there's a long path. But there's a short one, too. I'll teach it to you, if you'd like."

Milarepa became the best student Marpa ever had. He medi-tated, learned the secret teachings, and practiced them in his life. Some of the ideas were simple ones still floating around today: don't forget where you came from; treat others the way you want them to treat you. Milarepa made great strides forward the day he mastered this truth: if you want to walk through a gateway, hold the door open for others first.

Many people believe that when the student is ready, the teacher appears. Milarepa's understanding was that when the teacher appears, it's because we're ready to wake up and listen to the teacher inside ourselves. Milarepa's internal teacher was awakened. So was the deeper lama within, the part in each of us that has the ability to be aware and continue to learn.

Eventually Milarepa left Marpa to return to his homeland. He lived in the caves and fields, meditating and reminding people about karma, their power to make choices, and about how important their lives and choices are.

He didn't preach.

He sang.

He even forgave the aunt who helped steal his inheritance from him. He prayed for her enlightenment, too. "She doesn't owe me," Milarepa said. "I owe her everything I have. If it wasn't for her, I wouldn't be who and where I am. She helped steer me onto my path."

He realized that if he didn't have anyone to be angry with, he couldn't learn to forgive.

There is a reason everything happens, as our friend Milarepa learned. But sometimes it takes a long time and a series of painful, confusing experiences for us to see what that reason is.

By the time Milarepa died at age eighty-four, he was at one with the universe and himself. Some say that when he died, his physical body didn't deteriorate: he turned into a rainbow of light. His legend still lives today. He made and role-modeled the classic journey from sinner to saint.

"His songs reached even the dogs and the deer in the field," said a man who now lives in Tibet. "He helped the deer remember to stop being afraid and the dogs to stop chasing the deer."

Milarepa took the short path. He reached enlightenment in just one life. Then he taught others that it didn't have to take even that long. They could reach enlightenment by waking up, letting certain principles guide them, and making conscious choices in their lives each day.

We don't have to become gurus or live in caves and eat nettle soup to seek enlightenment, like Milarepa did. The problems that irritate and upset us most—the ones we're tempted to seek revenge for, throw money at, medicate, deny, go numb about, or try at all costs to avoid—aren't just problems. They're our mountain or cave in Tibet. They're disguised gateways to this path.

In my lifetime, I've seen a lot of changes in my life and in our world. There was a time when our choices were limited. Women were housewives, or got to choose between being a schoolteacher or a secretary for a career. Men were expected to earn the living. If abuse was going on, you shut up and took it. You bit the bullet. You got old. And when you got sick, you died.

Now cures have been found for many diseases, including viruses previously untreatable. Although a quarter of a million people die an early death each year, many people are living longer and in better health. That means we not only need to choose what we're going to do when we grow up; we may need to decide what we are going to do to earn a living again when we get old.

Information is at a premium, and choices abound. Do we use e-mail or the telephone, write a letter, or do we telepathically convey? We can communicate quickly and easily with people who are alive. Or we can visit a medium's talk show and communicate with people who are dead.

We can get married, live together, stay single, have an alternative or traditional lifestyle, have children, adopt children—whether we are single or married—create them in test tubes, or not have children, if that's our choice. We can get married, get divorced, then remarry again. We can get our face lifted, our cellulite lypoed. And not only can we get our hair cut off; with extensions and implants, they can now put it back on our heads.

Women can be with younger men, men can be with men, women can be with women; we can rent, buy, live in a mobile home, or walk away from it all and live in a tent. We can eat sugar or go sugar free; eat meat or not. And if we go vegetarian, we still have to choose. Are chicken, turkey, and fish considered vegetables or meat?

Options are available to us that we didn't have before: if we become overly and uncontrollably anxious and depressed, we can now chemically change our balance by taking a pill. Other choices are available to us, too—choices about how we can behave toward other people and ourselves—choices we didn't know about, way back when.

With all those hard calls and butterflies flapping their wings—and all the calculated and uncalculated risks—it's still the greatest thing we've got going.

Free will, baby. There's nothing else that even comes close on planet earth.

So what are you going to do?

You know the drill.

———

You get to choose.

Bibliography

Alcoholics Anonymous (The Big Book). New York: Alcoholics Anonymous World Services, 1976; Farber & Farber, 2001.

Andersen, Wes, and Owen Wilson. *The Royal Tenenbaums*. Directed by Wes Anderson. 2002. Motion picture.

Bach, Richard. *Jonathan Livingston Seagull*. New York: Scribner, 1970.

Beattie, Melody. *Codependent No More*. Center City, MN: Hazelden, 1986.

———. *Language of Letting Go*. Center City, MN: Hazelden, 1990.

Berg, Michael. *The Way*. New York: John Wiley & Sons, 2001.

Berg, Rabbi Phillip S. *Kabbalah for the Layman*. Vol. 2. New York and Jerusalem: Research Centre of Kabbalah, 1988.

———. *Kabbalah for the Layman*. Vol. 3. New York and Jerusalem: Research Centre of Kabbalah, 1988.

Berg, Rabbi Yehuda. *Power of Kabbalah*. Los Angeles: Kabbalah Centre International, 2000.

Bodine, Echo. *A Still, Small Voice*. Novato, CA: New World Library, 2001.

Campbell, Joseph. *The Hero's Journey.* San Francisco: Harper & Row, 1990.

China. 7th ed. Footscray, Victoria, Australia: Lonely Planet Publications, 2000.

Chödrön, Pema. *The Places That Scare You.* Boston and London: Shambhala, 2001.

———. *When Things Fall Apart.* Boston and London: Shambhala, 2000.

Cooper, J. California. *The Future Has a Past.* New York: Doubleday, 2000.

Crane, George. *Bones of the Master.* New York: Bantam Books, 2000.

Dossey, Larry, M.D. *Prayer Is Good Medicine.* San Francisco: Harper-SanFrancisco, 1996.

Edwards, Corinne. *Reflections from a Woman Alone.* Center City, MN: Hazelden, 2001.

Fielding, Helen. *Bridget Jones's Diary.* New York: Penguin Books, 2001.

Gantos, Jack. *Joey Pigza Swallowed the Key.* New York: Farrar, Straus & Giroux, 1998.

Gyatso, Geshe Kelsang Gyatso. *The Meditation Handbook.* London: Tharpa Publications, 1990.

His Holiness the Dalai Lama. *Ethics for the New Millenium.* New York: Riverhead Books, 1999.

His Holiness the Dalai Lama and Howard Cutler, M.D. *The Art of Happiness.* New York: Riverhead Books, 1998.

Hoffman, Lawrence A. *The Way into Jewish Prayer.* Woodstock, VT: Jewish Lights Publishing, 2000.

Jungreis, Rebbetzin Esther. *The Committed Life.* New York: Harper Perennial, 1998.

Kübler-Ross, Elisabeth. *The Tunnel and the Light.* New York: Marlowe & Company, 1999.

————. *The Wheel of Life*. New York: Touchstone/Simon & Schuster, 1997.

Kushner, Harold S. *When Bad Things Happen to Good People*. New York: Avon Books, 1981.

Lewis, C. S. *A Grief Observed*. New York: Bantam, 1976.

Lhalungpa, Lobsang P., trans. *The Life of Milarepa*. New York: Penguin/Arkana, 1992.

Lorenz, Edward N. "Deterministic Nonperiodic Flow." *Journal of Atmospheric Science* 20 (1963): 130–41.

Newton, Isaac. *Philosphiae naturalis principia mathematica* (Mathematical principles of natural philosophy), N.p., 1687.

Rieder, Marge. *Mission to Millboro*. Nevada City, CA: Blue Dolphin Publishing, 1993.

Rosanoff, Nancy. *The Complete Idiot's Guide to Making Money through Intuition*. New York: Alpha Books, 1999.

Schwartz, Jeffrey M., M.D., with Beverly Beyette. *Brain Lock*. New York: HarperCollins, 1997.

Seuss, Dr. *Oh, the Places You Will Go!* New York: Random House, 1990.

Telushkin, Rabbi Joseph. *The Book of Jewish Values*. New York: Bell Tower, 2000.

Wilkinson, Bruce. *The Prayer of Jabez*. Sisters, OR: Multnomah Publishers, 2000.

Williams, Margery. *The Velveteen Rabbit*. New York: Doubleday, 1922, 1991.

www.cosmicharmony.com/Av/Milarepa/Milarepa.htm

Acknowledgments

Thanks to:

Michael Bodine, for his unfailing and unwavering support and his Chinese handcuffs theory. *Choices* wouldn't have happened without him.

Emily Bump Girard for inspiring the idea for *Choices* with her article "Choose Your Own Adventure," published in the March 2001 issue of *Parachutist*.

My instructors Andy Delk in skydiving and Michael Fowler in aikido for teaching me about the concept of muscle memory in learning those sports, and Alcoholics Anonymous and Al-Anon for teaching me about the concept of muscle memory in learning about those programs.

Dan Cain, President of RS Eden in Minneapolis, for his beliefs in service, karma, and holding the door open for others.

Elisabeth Kübler-Ross—one of my true heroines.

Lori Teresa Yearwood and her father, Vernon Yearwood-Drayton.

Special thanks to Lami, Pat, Andy, Earnie Larsen, Joe, Corinne

Edwards, Debbie, Jeanie, Maragaret, Sherry, Debbi, and all the others who told their stories anonymously.

Family members Nichole, Michael, Julian, Maceo, Blake, Bianca, Katie, John, Ginette, Brandon, Courtney, Jeanne, Bob, Mom, Dad, Jim, Pam, Joanne, Donnie, and the rest.

David Vigliano, Louie, Liz, Steve, Anne—and all the people in the bookmaking industry who made this work possible.

Shane.

And God, who showed His face in each of the people mentioned above.

Index